M000084872

The enemy is attacking more aggressively these days because he knows that his time is short. Marilyn Hickey's new book, *Spiritual Warfare*, will give you the tools, the knowledge, and the practical experience you will need in the coming end times in order to have the total victory over the enemy of our souls. Read it, study it, and keep it by your side.

—*Yonggi Cho*
Chairman of the Board, Church Growth International

This book will teach you how to stand against the attacks of the evil one and become more than conquerors through Jesus who loves you. You don't have to live with the bondage of generational curses because the Lord Jesus can set you free. *Spiritual Warfare* can help set you free. Jesus wants you to live a happy life—free from demonic, harassing spirits. I pray that multitudes will read this book and be set free.

—*Dodie Osteen*
Cofounder, Lakewood Church

From the beginning of time, Satan's desire has been to defeat you and your family. Marilyn Hickey's book, *Spiritual Warfare*, prepares you for this battle by giving you the best weapon available—the Word of God. To draw on Marilyn's wisdom is wise counsel. I encourage you to prepare for the inevitable war by reading this training manual and preparing yourself to gain victory over your enemy.

—Tommy Barnett
Senior Pastor, Phoenix First Assembly of God

SPIRITUAL
WARFARE

SPIRITUAL
WARFARE

Protect Your Home from Spiritual Darkness

Marilyn HICKEY

WHITAKER
HOUSE

Unless otherwise indicated, all Scripture quotations are taken from the *New King James Version*, © 1979, 1980, 1982, 1984 by Thomas Nelson, Inc. Used by permission. All rights reserved. Scripture quotations marked (KJV) are taken from the King James Version of the Holy Bible. Scripture quotations marked (NASB) are taken from the updated *New American Standard Bible®*, NASB®, © 1960, 1962, 1963, 1968, 1971, 1972, 1973, 1975, 1977, 1995 by The Lockman Foundation. Used by permission. (www.Lockman.org)

Some definitions of Hebrew and Greek words are taken from *Strong's Exhaustive Concordance*.

Word definitions are taken from *Merriam-Webster's 11th Collegiate Dictionary* CD-ROM © 2003.

SPIRITUAL WARFARE:
Protect Your Home from Spiritual Darkness
Previously published as *Satan-Proof Your Home*

ISBN: 978-1-60374-224-5
Printed in the United States of America
© 1991, 2010 by Marilyn Hickey Ministries
P.O. Box 6598, Englewood, CO 80155

Whitaker House
1030 Hunt Valley Circle
New Kensington, PA 15068
www.whitakerhouse.com

Library of Congress Cataloging-in-Publication Data

Hickey, Marilyn.
  Spiritual warfare / by Marilyn Hickey.
      p. cm.
  Rev. ed. of: Satan-proof your home.
  Summary: "Equips readers to fight off the devil's attacks against their homes and families and to invoke the blessings of God by practicing scriptural principles and believing in faith that God will deliver unsaved loved ones"—Provided by publisher.
  ISBN 978-1-60374-224-5 (trade pbk. : alk. paper) 1. Spiritual warfare. I. Hickey, Marilyn. Satan-proof your home. II. Title.
  BV4509.5.H53 2010
  235'.4—dc22
                                                                                      2010013097

No part of this book may be reproduced or transmitted in any form or by any means electronic or mechanical—including photocopying, recording, or by any information storage and retrieval system—without permission in writing from the publisher. Please direct your inquiries to permissionseditor@whitakerhouse.com.

2 3 4 5 6 7 8 9 10 11 **WH** 17 16 15 14 13 12 11 10

CONTENTS

1. Satan-Proofing Your Home 11

2. Preparing for Battle 33

3. Bless Your Household 57

4. Come Out of the Closet 81

5. Mark Your Household 105

6. Sowing and Reaping Miracles 127

7. Wisdom for Your Future 149

8. Turn on the Light! 173

9. Getting God's Priorities 193

10. Transforming Power 215

About the Author 237

Chapter One

Satan-Proofing Your Home

Wouldn't it be wonderful to know that your home was totally secure and not vulnerable to any attack of Satan? We *know* how bold he can be—why, he'll barge right in without even bothering to knock!

Some people believe that Christians never have struggles, but that's a lie. Satan's not just trying to destroy God's kingdom or the church—he's after Christian families, too! If you haven't taken precautions to guard your home against Satan's divisive elements, your family won't withstand the force of his storms—it will crash.

Millions of families are facing failure all over the world. The "failure of the family" phenomenon indiscriminately affects a wide cross section of homes. It ignores race, financial status, religious beliefs, and other demographic distinctions, and it leaves behind a tragic trail of emptiness, bitterness, and despair.

I believe God may have had families in mind when He said, *"My people are destroyed for lack of knowledge"* (Hosea 4:6). Sure, many powerful, demonic forces are contributing to the destruction of the family—some have been undermining the family unit for decades.

But God did *not* say that we would be destroyed by demonic forces.

Satan is attacking today's families because we have fallen prey to one of his most subtle devices: our own lack of knowledge. The apostle Paul wrote, *"Lest Satan should take advantage of us; for we are not ignorant of his devices"* (2 Corinthians 2:11).

You can Satan-proof your home so that the next time the devil comes near your loved ones, you'll know how to stop him dead in his tracks!

LAY THE RIGHT FOUNDATION

Of course, you cannot stand effectively against the devil on behalf of your loved ones until you have laid the right foundation—Satan-proofing yourself. You must practice what you'll preach.

Therefore whoever hears these sayings of Mine, and does them, I will liken him to a wise man who built his house on the rock: and the rain descended, the floods came, and the winds blew and beat on that house; and it did not fall, for it was founded on the rock. But everyone who hears these sayings of Mine, and does not do them, will be like a foolish man who built his house on the sand: and the rain descended, the floods came, and the winds blew and beat on that house; and

SATAN-PROOFING YOUR HOME

it fell. And great was its fall.

(Matthew 7:24–27)

Your foundation must be built upon a rock. The Bible says that Jesus Christ is the Rock of our salvation:

And all drank the same spiritual drink. For they drank of that spiritual Rock that followed them, and that Rock was Christ. (1 Corinthians 10:4)

He shall cry to Me, "You are my Father, My God, and the rock of my salvation." (Psalm 89:26)

I receive hundreds of letters each week from people all over the country. Many people write to share the terrible consequences of putting their confidence in something or someone other than Jesus Christ.

One courageous woman shared:

I was hooked on crack, and walked the streets of Daytona Beach collecting aluminum cans to pay for my habit. I lived with crooks, thieves, and prostitutes—and I was all of these. I am an educated woman with a master's degree, and I once had held a $50,000-a-year job. But I did not know Jesus—cocaine was my choice.

Cocaine had become this woman's god, and it had almost destroyed her. Eventually, she had been born again and returned to her parents' home, and God had begun nurturing her to spiritual health. She had taken

13

the first step to Satan-proofing her home by Satan-proofing herself, and she'd become a dynamic witness to her family. Since she wrote her first letter to me, her older brother has been set free from a destructive lifestyle of drug addiction. He now lives with her, and they are praising the Lord together.

Friends, there is absolutely no question that if you put your hope into anything or anyone less than Jesus, you are building your future on sand, and you will eventually fall into destruction.

ERECT A STRONG STRUCTURE

After your eternal life has been established *solidly* in Christ Jesus, the next step toward Satan-proofing your home is to structure your life on the godly principles contained in God's Word.

In my ministry magazine, *Outpouring*, I descibe a plan that enables you to read through the Bible in one year. We have received many testimonies from all kinds of people who have been blessed by following this plan and reading through the Bible each year. My heart was touched by a teenage girl who wrote:

> I think it is beneficial for teenagers to read through the Bible. When I first started, it was like I had to make myself read it every day. But once I had established it as a discipline, it got easier. I don't expect some big revelation every

day; I just try to understand what it's really saying...and stick with it because in the long run,
it will pay off.

This believer's faith has been founded in Jesus Christ,
and now she is Satan-proofing herself by studying the
Bible. When she is confronted by temptations or trials,
her response will be structured based on God's Word.

You know, it's curious that both the houses discussed in Matthew 7:24–27 were subjected to the same
type of storm. Some of you probably think that your life
was supposed to automatically become immune to the
attacks of the enemy when you were born again. Some
of you probably think that your level of spirituality determines whether or not you are attacked by the devil.
But it simply isn't so.

Of course, being a mature Christian certainly will
give you a tremendous edge over the devil. But the
simple fact remains that whether you are a saint or
a sinner, a new Christian or a mature believer, Satan
will throw his fiery darts at you. Why? Satan hates
God; therefore, he also hates people, because we were
created in God's image:

> So God created man in His own image;...and
> God said to them, "Be fruitful and multiply; fill
> the earth and subdue it."   (Genesis 1:27–28)

The Hebrew word used here for *subdue* means "to
tread down, to conquer, to bring into bondage." It's
God's will for people to bear fruit and to subdue the

> *It's God's will for people to bear fruit and to subdue the earth. But, first, we must renew our minds and be conformed to the image of Christ.*

earth. But, first, we must renew our minds and be conformed to the image of Christ. (See Romans 8:29; 12:2.)

The major thing you will discover as you study your Bible is that Jesus is a *winner*. And, when you structure your life upon the godly principles that He taught in the Scriptures, you will become a winner, too!

In Christ, believers have the power to tread on the devil.

*Behold, I give unto you power to **tread** on serpents and scorpions, and over all the power of the enemy: and nothing shall by any means hurt you.* (Luke 10:19 KJV, emphasis added)

In Christ, believers are more than conquerors.

*Yet in all these things we are **more than conquerors** through Him who loved us.*
(Romans 8:37, emphasis added)

In Christ, believers have the authority to bind and loose.

*Assuredly, I say to you, whatever you **bind** on earth will be **bound** in heaven, and whatever*

*you **loose** on earth will be **loosed** in heaven.*
(Matthew 18:18, emphasis added)

When you begin to walk fully according to the purpose and in the power given to you by God, you will be able to Satan-proof your home and keep the devil from ripping off your loved ones.

You must learn to stop listening to the devil's lies! God does not want your marriage to end prematurely because of the death of your spouse or because of divorce. God does not want your family members tormented in relationships that are physically, mentally, emotionally, or sexually abusive. God does not want your family members to fall into sin and become hooked on drugs and alcohol, adultery, pornography, or just plain "riotous living." God does not want your finances to be in such turmoil that your family suffers neglect because you have to work day and night to make ends meet. No, He most certainly does not!

God has predestined you, His child, to be conformed into the image of Jesus (See Romans 8:29.) Remember; Jesus is a winner, and, through Him, you and your family can be winners, too!

> *Remember; Jesus is a winner, and, through Him, you and your family can be winners, too!*

Although the enemy will try to divide and conquer your household, you can stop him from devastating your lives and Satan-proof your home by taking a stand for your family.

PUT THE WORD INTO ACTION

I noticed something about those two houses in Matthew. The first house had been Satan-proofed—it was rooted by faith in Jesus and structured on God's Word.

And the rain descended, the floods came, and the winds blew and beat on that house; and it did not fall, for it was founded on the rock.
(Matthew 7:25)

The second house, on the other hand, was built on sand, which can represent something or someone other than Christ and solid Bible doctrine.

Every one that heareth these sayings of mine, and doeth them not, shall be likened unto a foolish man, which built his house upon the sand: and the rain descended, and the floods came, and the winds blew, and beat upon that house; and it fell: and great was the fall of it.
(Matthew 7:26–27)

Both houses were subjected to the same storm; however, though the first house may have swayed and bent under the ferocity of the winds and rains, it did not fall. By contrast, the second house had not been Satan-proofed; it had been built on sand. It couldn't handle the pressure of the storm, and it was destroyed.

Since God wants our families to be Satan-proofed, let's dig deeper to find out what it takes to be a Satan-proofer. We know without a doubt that being born again is essential and reading the Bible is necessary. But knowing Jesus as our Savior and being aware of godly principles are simply the first steps toward defending ourselves and our loved ones against Satan's tactics.

Satan-proofers are believers who have taken charge by letting godly principles become alive in their circumstances. They have stepped out of the comfort zone of merely *hearing* God's Word and into the battle zone of actively *doing* what God's Word instructs us to do. James 1:22 admonishes us, *"But be doers of the word, and not hearers only, deceiving yourselves."*

> **Satan-proofers are believers who have taken charge by letting godly principles become alive in their circumstances.**

The Bible gives us much more than the steps to eternal life; it also provides step-by-step instructions for living in the world every day. When you really get into studying your Bible regularly, you'll be able to Satan-proof your home as you begin to *act* on the Word of God that is within you. Some people read the Bible over and over again but fail to apply its divine principles to their everyday lives. The Word has worked for people since Bible times, and the Word will work in your life, too!

In order to take a stand upon godly principles, a believer first needs to develop a trusting relationship with God. That way, when the storms of life come, a Satan-proofer can say, "God, I trust You, and I'm going to stand on what Your Word says. I know You are faithful, and You will not fail me."

This type of intimacy between God and man evolves out of a consistent, committed prayer life. A Satan-proofer regularly spends time in God's presence praying, worshipping, praising, fasting, studying, and meditating. A Satan-proofer knows and trusts God to the utmost.

Your relationship with God, based on the rock-solid foundation of Jesus Christ, is what will always hold you steady when you are battling the enemy for yourself and your family.

BE A GAP-STANDER, NOT A GAP-FINDER

Satan-proofing your home requires you to be a *gap-stander*. When I think about standing in the gap for my family, I think about Abraham—he spent time in God's presence, and God established a personal relationship with him. I get so encouraged when I look at the relationship between Abraham and God. It was so intimate. The Bible says that Abraham *"was called the friend of God"* (James 2:23). Scripture also indicates that God *trusted* Abraham enough to reveal to him His plans regarding the coming judgment upon the wicked twin cities of Sodom and Gomorrah.

> *And the LORD said, "Shall I hide from Abraham what I am doing?...Because the outcry against Sodom and Gomorrah is great, and because their sin is very grave, I will go down now and see whether they have done altogether according to the outcry against it that has come to Me; and if not, I will know."* (Genesis 18:17, 20–21)

These people were really the pits! They were involved in all kinds of things, like terrible sexual sins. Some of those awful Sodomite men even demanded that Abraham's nephew, Lot, turn over to them the two angels whom God had sent to confirm their wicked activities so that they could have sex with them! So, God said, "That's enough!" And He destroyed them.

Prior to that, we see God actually conferring with Abraham about His plans to bring judgment upon Sodom and Gomorrah. How did Abraham react? Certainly, he was concerned, because Lot and his family lived in Sodom. Let's see—did Abraham go running to Sarah to tell her what God was going to do? Did Abraham start whining to his friends, "Oh, what shall I do? Something awful is going to happen; please pray for my family"? Did Abraham get nervous and start biting his nails or pulling out his hair?

No! Abraham began to talk with God on behalf of Lot and his family. Abraham began to Satan-proof his family through intercessory prayer:

> [Abraham asked God,] *"Suppose there were fifty righteous within the city; would You also destroy the place and not spare it for the fifty righteous that were in it?"...So the* LORD *said, "If I find in Sodom fifty righteous within the city, then I will spare all the place for their sakes."*
>
> (Genesis 18:24, 26)

Abraham kept right on negotiating until God agreed to spare the city even if there were only ten righteous people living in it. (See verses 27–32.) Can you imagine it? The people of Sodom and Gomorrah were so wicked that there were not even ten good people in the entire city.

I think Abraham probably stopped at ten because he thought that there had to be at least ten good people in Sodom. After all, there were six in Lot's family—Lot, his wife, and his two daughters and their husbands. Abraham had no idea that Lot's two sons-in-law would reject God's offer, or that Lot's wife would turn from God, too. Abraham was certain that God would find four more people who had not been overtaken by the terrible sin that was running rampant in that area.

I wonder how I would respond if God suddenly said, "Marilyn, because of the homosexuality, prostitution, and drug abuse in Anywhere, USA, I am going to wipe it off the face of the earth." How would you respond? Some Christians probably would cheer God on and say, "Go ahead, God! We need to get some of these sinners out of here!" But what if you had relatives living in that city? Would you feel the same way?

No matter how terrible the place, I believe God would expect us to be merciful and try to save the city, if for no other reason than the fact that our families were there.

The wise woman builds her house, but the foolish pulls it down with her hands.

(Proverbs 14:1)

I believe prayer is one way in which the wise woman in Proverbs 14:1 stood in the gap and Satan-proofed her home. The foolish woman, on the other hand, pulled her house down with her own hands. Perhaps, instead of praying, she just pointed her finger at everyone's mistakes while her family crumbled under the weight of Satan's attacks.

You know, if we took a survey and asked Christians whether they considered themselves to be gap-standers or gap-finders, I am reasonably certain that most of them probably would answer, "Gap-stander." Yet, the statistics on the breakdown of marriages show that both Christian and non-Christian families are falling apart at similar rates.

Friends, this is a cold, hard truth with which we need to come to grips. Most Christians have allowed themselves to become foolish by pointing a finger rather than pointing a prayer. And while we have been busy focusing on the greatness of sin instead of the greatness of God, the devil has been running off merrily with everything that we hold dear.

But I want to encourage you—there is hope! It is not too late for Christians to turn this awful trend around and take a stand against the destruction the devil has planned for our families.

> **God is for families! He doesn't want your family to be destroyed by any of the horrendous things that come out of the devil's devious mind.**

God is for families! He doesn't want your family to be destroyed by any of the horrendous things that come out of the devil's devious mind. No, God wants you to become an intercessor and to Satan-proof your family with effective, fervent prayer.

You see, God is omniscient (all-knowing). God knew before He ever shared His plans with Abraham that he would stand in the gap for Lot. It didn't matter to Abraham that Lot was a loser; he prayed for him anyway. That's why God allows you to know some "not so nice" things about your family, too. He doesn't want you to point your finger and condemn; instead, God wants you to pray and stop what the devil is trying to do to your loved ones.

It's up to us to pray for our families—to keep them before God. Who is going to do it if we don't? You say, "Well, I think the church should." But God wants *you* to stand in the gap for your own family.

I just love the way God works when He has gap-standers who are willing to Satan-proof their loved ones. Abraham could have chosen to be a gap finder and said, "I didn't want Lot to move down there, but he insisted. And Lot didn't just stay out on the plains where he had pitched his tent; he *lived* in Sodom. That's where his girls went to school, and he and his wife had an active social life. Why, Lot even sits at the city gate with the other civic leaders. You know, God, Lot may be family, but Lot really is not so swift. So, go ahead and wipe out Sodom. I'll understand."

Of course, we know Abraham didn't say any of that. Instead, he stood in the gap for Lot with prayer. Abraham didn't think God was going to destroy Sodom and Gomorrah, so imagine how his faith fell when he got up the next morning and *"looked toward Sodom and Gomorrah, and toward all the land of the plain; and he saw, and behold, the smoke of the land which went up like the smoke of a furnace"* (Genesis 19:28).

When Abraham saw all that smoke rising, I'm sure he probably thought, *Oh, dear God, dear God, what about Lot? You couldn't find even ten?* Then, sadly, Abraham became discouraged because the outward manifestation of God's answer to his prayer wasn't quite what he expected it to be.

It's easy to become discouraged when we pray and pray for our families. My husband and I have been praying for our relatives for years. Some of them have gotten saved, and others of them have gone from bad to worse. But we are going to keep on praying because

God's Word has been formed on the inside of us, and we are holding on to His promises.

Abraham let go of God's promises and completely blew it.

> *And Abraham journeyed from there to the South,*
> *and dwelt between Kadesh and Shur, and stayed*
> *in Gerar. Now Abraham said of Sarah his wife,*
> *"She is my sister." And Abimelech king of Gerar*
> *sent and took Sarah. But God came to Abimelech*
> *in a dream by night, and said to him, "Indeed*
> *you are a dead man because of the woman whom*
> *you have taken, for she is a man's wife."*
>
> (Genesis 20:1–3)

Abraham was afraid that Lot had been killed. Now, I am sure that many of you have gotten out of whack, too, when things haven't turned out as you thought they should have. I certainly have, and, like Abraham did, I've tried to back away from God's plan for my life.

Abraham had gotten out of God's will and into fear. He ended up telling Sarah to lie about being his wife and almost got Abimelech killed. Things really got pretty messy for a while until God corrected the situation and put Abraham back on the right track. But if Abraham had not judged God's faithfulness according to his own agenda, he never would have become discouraged and taken this dumb detour down to Gerar, anyway.

When we are Satan-proofing our homes, it is important that we not become discouraged and give up just

26

because things aren't progressing in the way we think they should. We have to stick to the Word and believe that God will work out His will in whatever situation our loved ones are facing.

And don't forget the wise woman in Proverbs 14:1 who built up rather than tore down: *"The wise woman builds her house, But the foolish tears it down with her own hands"* (NASB). If you keep in mind that your enemy is the devil and not other people, you'll never tear your family apart. Rather, you'll always zero in on Satan and tear him apart instead.

Years ago, before my children were born, my husband, Wally, was severely depressed. He became moody and sometimes wouldn't talk to me for two or three days at a time, and I just hated it. I would try to talk to him, but he would say, "I'm a failure. Please don't talk to me; don't bother me."

I honestly didn't know what to do, but I heard the Word of God, which had formed on the inside of me, and it promises that the Holy Spirit will pray for things beyond our understanding. So, I thought, *I'm going to stop whining around and being mad at Wally. I have the Word inside me, and I am going to act like the Word works by taking a stand on it.*

So, for one hour, I prayed in tongues, and God showed me what to do. I sat down and began to go through the Scriptures with Wally, reminding him that he could not possibly be a failure because the Bible says that believers will always triumph in Christ. (See 2 Corinthians 2:14.)

At first, Wally just wanted me to leave him alone, but I continued challenging him and insisting that he respond. Finally, he started to laugh, and the depression broke. That was more than three decades ago, and Wally hasn't been severely depressed since.

I stood in the gap and Satan-proofed my home by *acting* on God's Word inside of me. I spoke the Word, and the devil had to stop attacking my husband with depression.

SPEAK THE WORD OF GOD

The Bible says that God's Word is a sword.

And take the helmet of salvation, and the sword of the Spirit, which is the word of God.
(Ephesians 6:17)

For the word of God is living and powerful, and sharper than any two-edged sword, piercing even to the division of soul and spirit, and of joints and marrow, and is a discerner of the thoughts and intents of the heart.   (Hebrews 4:12)

Someone once told me about a Spirit-filled man whom I'll call Tom. He had been praying for his sister, who was hooked on drugs and involved in all kinds of immorality. She lived a very sinful life. One weekend, while their mother was away, the sister went out

28

and didn't come home until 6:30 the next morning. She brought some athletic-looking guy home with her, and they went into her mother's bedroom.

Tom was almost overwhelmed when he asked God what to do, and God told him, "Throw the guy out!" Tom went into his mother's bedroom, told his sister to put her clothes on, and asked her boyfriend, "How would you feel if your sister brought some guy home to sleep with her in your mother's bed? Would you like it?" The boyfriend responded, "No." Tom told him to get dressed and leave, and the guy did just that. His sister was absolutely furious.

When Tom left home to go back to school, he began to Satan-proof his sister: He stood in the gap and spoke for his sister, saying, "Satan, you can't have any part of my sister. Adultery, you can't have a part of my sister. Drugs, you can't have a part of my sister." Tom continued this for exactly three months. Then, one day, his sister showed up at his door, saying, "I want to get saved." The Word of God had cut through all the junk in her life and had turned her completely around!

God's Word discerns the thoughts and intents of the heart. So, when we pray God's Word, using it on spirits and

When we pray God's Word, using it on spirits and situations, it begins to cut through thoughts and attitudes in order to bring about a change.

situations, it begins to cut through thoughts and attitudes in order to bring about a change.

Instead of complaining and allowing any "*corrupt
word*" (Ephesians 4:29) to come out of our mouths about
how poorly other people are doing, we literally need to
speak to their spirits by name. We need to say, for example, "Susie [or whoever], you're not going to drink
alcohol or do drugs." Then, Satan-proof the person by
speaking directly to the enemy, saying, "Devil, you're
not going to put alcoholism or drug addiction on Susie
[or whomever]."

I believe that when we begin to speak and continue
to speak with persistence to the spirits involved, we
will crack some things wide open. Why? Because our
foundation is in Jesus, the living Word.

> *They overcame him by the blood of the Lamb,
> and by the word of their testimony.*
> (Revelation 12:11)

We can Satan-proof our loved ones by cutting through
some of the garbage in their lives so they can hear the
Holy Spirit and then come through with flying colors!

So, you see, being a Satan-proofer is more than just
knowing Jesus and being aware of what God's Word
says. A Satan-proofer literally takes the Word and chops
off the devil's head with it.

Why don't you begin *right now* to be wise like the
woman in Proverbs 14:1 and build up your loved ones
through intercessory prayer?

Women, I believe you can Satan-proof your husbands, for example, by speaking the Word over their clothes while you're ironing or putting clean sheets on your bed. Try praying, "I thank You, Father, because no weapon formed against my husband shall prosper, and everything that rises against him shall fall." I think that something powerful happens in the home when a woman prays like that. You can prevent violent crimes from occurring in your home, and you can put strife on the run!

Men, you can Satan-proof your wives by speaking to their spirits, for example, "Mary [or whoever], you will never be a nag. You will always be sweet because you have the peace of God, which passes all understanding."

Parents, you can speak God's Word concerning obedience into your children's spirits by telling them they will never be rebellious and affirming how smart they are in school because they have the mind of Christ. Then, speak with authority to the devil. Tell Satan that he will never get your family because you are standing in the gap for them, in the name of Jesus.

Finally, I cannot emphasize enough the importance of praying in the Holy Spirit. The Bible says, "*But you, beloved, building yourselves up on your most holy faith, praying in the Holy Spirit, keep yourselves in the love of God, looking for the mercy of our Lord Jesus Christ unto eternal life*" (Jude 20–21).

Now, let me ask you, what do you think would happen if you began to walk around your house or workplace praying in the Spirit? You don't have to make a big fuss;

you can pray in the Spirit on the inside, in silence, and no one will know what you are doing but God.

> **Praying in the Spirit will keep you in the love of God, and I believe that praying in the Spirit also will keep you in love with one another.**

Praying in the Spirit will keep you in the love of God, and I believe that praying in the Spirit also will keep you in love with one another. So, when your spouse, children, or parents get out of line, you should lovingly pray for and Satan-proof them. The Holy Spirit will keep you in God's perfect love, and you will be acting in a way that will bring God's mercy into whatever situation Satan may try to bring against your home.

Chapter Two

Preparing for Battle

W e are going to look at some practical steps to Satan-proofing our families, and I am going to put a lot of emphasis on the power of the Holy Spirit. When you become a bona fide Satan-proofer, you will need the power of God, because what you actually are doing is declaring war on Satan. You're saying an emphatic **no** to the destructive plans he has concocted to bring division and strife into your family. In order to succeed at stopping the devil, it is imperative that you move in the power of the Holy Spirit.

If there is anyplace where we need to be led of the Holy Spirit, it's in the privacy of our own homes. There really is a lot of stress in most home situations. You may have heard the saying, "The boss strikes out at you, you go home and strike out at your spouse, your spouse strikes out at the kids, and the kids strike out at the poor dog!" Even though that sounds humorous, it is basically what happens in many family units—and the reality isn't humorous.

We probably do not intend to hurt our family members; nevertheless, as sinful humans, we often tend to strike out and hurt those who are closest to us. However, when your boss gets on your nerves, if your family has been Satan-proofed by the presence of the Holy Spirit, then you won't go home after work and take it out on your spouse, your children, or your dog. The Holy Spirit will help you work out your emotional frustration before you cause trouble for your family.

Many wives are probably saying, "Marilyn, you don't know my husband—he's as mean as a snake!" Many of you other wives may have become so critical of your husbands that you just nag, nag, nag the poor guys, though they're trying as hard as they can to please you. There are others of you whose children have just about driven you up the wall. So, what do you do? You pray in the Holy Spirit (without letting anyone else hear you), and God will help you to respond to your family in love—even when they are being unloving toward you.

> *Your family life will be a lot less stressful if you Satan-proof your relationships with your children by allowing the Holy Spirit to lead you in child rearing.*

There is often a great deal of tension between parents and children. Yet, you'll find that your family life will be a lot less stressful if you Satan-proof your relationships with your children by allowing the Holy Spirit to lead you in child rearing.

There is a lot of tension between parents and children in today's society. You'll find that your family life will be a lot less stressful if you Satan-proof your relationships with your children by allowing the Holy Spirit to lead you in child rearing.

COMMAND YOUR CHILDREN TO SERVE GOD

One of the first things the Holy Spirit will lead you to do concerning your children is to raise them to serve God. Do you remember what God said about Abraham? He said, *"He will command his children and his household after him"* (Genesis 18:19 KJV).

God was saying that Abraham would raise his children to serve the Lord. God must have had a lot of confidence in Abraham, because He spoke these words long before Abraham and Sarah's child of promise, Isaac, was born. That was quite a compliment! What about your household? What would God say about your child-rearing techniques? Could He say that you are raising your children up to serve Him?

Maybe you raised your children according to God's Word, but they still went the way of the world and fell into a destructive lifestyle. I understand how you feel. My son got involved in drugs as a teenager. But I knew that I had raised him to serve the Lord, and I refused to measure the truth of God's Word according to my son's lifestyle. I knew that my son Michael's life was going to line up with what God said about him. The Bible said it, and I believed it with all my heart. Today, I'm pleased to report that Michael is a grown man and has been free of drugs and alcohol for a long time. He has been reconciled to our family and is a great blessing to us.

Parents are supposed to plant the seed of God's Word in the hearts of their children. We are to teach them the Bible and keep them exposed to a godly lifestyle by setting a good example. But as far as serving the Lord is concerned, that happens only when their hearts have been changed—a work of the Holy Spirit.

After expressing His confidence that Abraham would command his children to serve Him, God vowed to keep His promises to Abraham:

> *For I know him, that he will command his children and his household after him, and they shall keep the way of the LORD, to do justice and judgment; that the LORD may bring upon Abraham that which he hath spoken of him.*
>
> (Genesis 18:19 KJV)

The Holy Spirit drew Isaac unto God, and the Holy Spirit will draw your child, also. As the Bible says, *"Train up a child in the way he should go, and when he is old he will not depart from it"* (Proverbs 22:6).

One time, we received a touching letter from a prisoner who had read my book *A Cry for Miracles*. He said that he was a Vietnam War veteran and had been experiencing terrible inner conflict because he had killed people during the war: As a child, he had been taught in Sunday school that it was wrong to kill. After the war, his wife and daughter had drowned tragically in a boating accident. He said that he hadn't been able to take it anymore, and he'd simply "lost it." He'd become addicted to drugs, had written phony prescriptions for codeine, and eventually had ended up in prison. "I just thought there was no hope for me," he wrote. "I had been in despair until I read that book. Out of the blackness of where I was, I began to see a little pinpoint of light.

His letter was full of hope, and he said that he intended to go to the prison chaplain to ask for prayer. When I read his letter, I thought, *Wow! Somebody way back in his Lutheran background got the Word into him and probably prayed for him.* Someone had Satan-proofed this man as a child, and although he had detoured and suffered through so many terrible experiences, that precious seed had taken root and was now beginning to sprout.

Folks, we are to bring our children up according to God's Word. And, by faith, we must *know* that God will manifest His will in their lives, despite what the outward circumstances may look like.

We Christians begin to Satan-proof our children when we dedicate them in church and bring them to Sunday school. When we do that, I believe that God's

> **God dispatches angels to go before and behind our children not only to protect them but also to cause their lives to stay in line with His Word.**

supernatural hand comes upon our children. And then God dispatches angels to go before and behind our children not only to protect them but also to cause their lives to stay in line with His Word.

So what if everything doesn't turn out the way we think it should in our children's lives? There will come a time when God's all-powerful Holy Spirit will draw our children to God through Jesus Christ. I have watched it happen again and again.

I want you to notice that God didn't say Abraham gave his household the *option* of whether or not to serve God. We can't say to our children, "Well, honey, if you like the Bible, then you can read it. But if you don't, well, you don't have to read it, because I want you to grow up with the freedom to choose." No! God said that Abraham would *command* his family to serve the Lord. The word *command* means "to direct authoritatively: order; to exercise a dominating influence over: have command of," according to *Merriam-Webster's 11th Collegiate Dictionary*. We are to direct and order our children to keep the ways of the Lord if we want the blessings of God to follow them.

God told Abraham's son Isaac, *"I will perform the oath which I swore to Abraham your father"* (Genesis 26:3). Abraham's grandson Jacob also eventually came to serve God and came under the same covenantal promises: *"The land which I gave Abraham and Isaac I give to you; and to your descendants after you I give this land"* (Genesis 35:12).

Wise parents raise their children to line up their lives according to God's Word. When we speak the Word to them, we can be certain that God's Word will not return void but will accomplish God's purposes for it. (See Isaiah 55:11.) Although your children may get out of God's will and stray into sinful lifestyles, God will cultivate the godly seed you have planted in their lives. The Holy Spirit will continue to draw them until they turn their lives back toward God.

Give Spiritual Instruction

If you want your children to be influenced by the Holy Spirit, it's necessary that you first set a personal example.

Look at Joshua. He led the children of Israel into Canaan, and they took the Promised Land in six and a half years. Joshua was a powerhouse for God, and he was definitely full of the Holy Spirit, as affirmed by Numbers 27:18: *"And the Lord said to Moses: 'Take Joshua the son of Nun with you, a man in whom is the Spirit, and lay your hand on him.'"*

I know Joshua's children were influenced by his spiritual walk with God because, at the end of his life, he spoke these words:

> *And if it seems evil to you to serve the LORD, choose for yourselves this day whom you will*

39

> *serve, whether the gods which your fathers served*
> *that were on the other side of the River, or the*
> *gods of the Amorites, in whose land you dwell.*
> *But as for me and my house, we will serve the*
> LORD.   (Joshua 24:15)

Joshua was determined to stand in the gap for his family by vowing that they would continue to serve God after he died. He had Satan-proofed his family by commanding them according to God's Word, and he had led them as he had been led by the Holy Spirit.

Did you know that the Holy Spirit will instruct you in how you should discipline your children? I met a woman in Chicago—she had came to pick me up at the airport when I arrived for one of my Bible Encounters—who told me as we drove along that she was a single parent. When her son had reached his teenage years, he'd become wild and rebellious. The woman had been a Christian for only a couple of years, and she'd thought, *Oh, God, what am I going to do with this boy? I don't have a husband to really line him up, and he's going through these difficult years. What shall I do?*

The Holy Spirit had said to her, "Every time he disobeys or gets into rebellion, have him write down all the Scriptures on disobedience and all the Scriptures on obedience." So, she'd taken her topical Bible and showed her son where all of those Scriptures could be found, then had told him to write them all down *in longhand.*

Every time her son was disobedient or rebellious, she made him write down all those Scriptures. He spent hours and hours writing pages and pages, and do you know what? Writing all those Scripture verses absolutely cured him! After a while, he stopped rebelling and really got turned on to God's Word. He began to serve the Lord and even attended Bible school!

By obeying the specific instructions given to her by the Holy Spirit, this woman Satan-proofed her son and protected him from the devil's disgusting attempts to bury him in a lifestyle of rebellion and disobedience.

The Bible includes God's specific instructions on child rearing to a couple who lived in Zorah in the thirteenth chapter of Judges. Manoah and his wife didn't have any children because she was barren. One day, while Manoah's wife was out in the field, an angel appeared to her and said, "You're going to have a baby boy." Of course, she was excited and ran to tell her husband what the angel had said. Manoah listened to his wife but wanted to hear the message straight from the angel's mouth. *"Then Manoah prayed to the Lord, and said, 'O my Lord, please let the Man of God whom You sent come to us again and teach us what we shall do for the child who will be born'"* (Judges 13:8).

The angel told them that the boy was to be raised a Nazarite, which meant he was never to touch anything dead, drink wine, or cut his hair. The angel also repeated his earlier instructions to Manoah's wife: while she was pregnant, she was not to eat anything that came from the vine, including wine and strong drink, nor could she eat any unclean thing. (See verse 14.)

This boy, of course, was Samson, and the Bible says that the Spirit of the Lord *"began to move upon him at Mahaneh Dan between Zorah and Eshtaol"* (Judges 13:25). Samson had an unusual anointing on him, and although he certainly took a few detours, eventually accomplished God's purpose for his life and destroyed many of Israel's enemies. (See Judges 16:30.) But before the Spirit of the Lord came upon Samson, God had already done a work in the hearts of his parents.

It was the same way with Joshua. Remember that he said, *"As for me and my house, we will serve the Lord"* (Joshua 24:15). Where did God begin working first? In Joshua's heart. It is important for us parents to understand that God wants to begin working in our hearts first, and then He will work in the hearts of our children.

I want to encourage you because some of you may be feeling like flops and failures as parents. I know how you feel because I've felt the same way—most of us, at one time or another, probably have felt that way. We've thought, *God, I'm no good at parenting. I'm not sure You should have given me any children. I don't know which way to turn.*

God doesn't mind when you get to the point where you don't know what to do next. Usually, that's when you start looking toward Him and asking for direction. It probably would be a lot easier on everyone if you would make a habit of seeking His instruction in every phase of child rearing. We can be assured that, just as God answered Manoah's prayer for direction in raising Samson, He also will answer you when you seek His direction for your children.

God doesn't mind when you get to the point where you don't know what to do next. Usually, that's when you start looking toward Him and asking for direction.

As I said earlier, this chapter has a strong emphasis on the Holy Spirit operating in our homes. Some of you may be wondering, *Who is the Holy Spirit, where is the Holy Spirit, and how can I be instructed by the Holy Spirit?*

> *Do you not know that you are the temple of God and that the Spirit of God dwells in you?*
> (1 Corinthians 3:16)

The Holy Spirit is the third member of the Trinity, along with the Father and the Son. The Holy Spirit is God, and if you are a born-again believer, the Holy Spirit lives inside your spirit.

There are many names in the Bible that describe different attributes of God. One of them is *El Shaddai*, which means "the God who is more than enough." Job really got a revelation of El Shaddai when he lost his family, his health, and his wealth, and then the God who is more than enough restored everything to him in double portion. (See Job 42:12.) Abraham and Sarah encountered *El Shaddai* when the God who is more than enough opened Sarah's barren womb and she conceived a son, Isaac, despite the fact that she and her husband were long past childbearing age. (See Genesis 21:1–3.)

> **The Holy Spirit is the Spirit of God who is more than enough, and He has made Himself available to you.**

The Holy Spirit is the Spirit of God who is more than enough, and He has made Himself available to you. When you don't have the answers for the many, many circumstances that come against your family, just remember that the Spirit of the living God is waiting with fail-safe instructions to direct you through any situation you're facing.

How does He instruct you? Sometimes, God will give you visions. I haven't had many visions—there are probably about three that I can recall—but the ones I've had were wonderful. Most of the instructions that I've received from the Holy Spirit have come like impressions from deep in my spirit. But, sometimes, the Holy Spirit will instruct you with a Scripture, and your answer will become clearer to you as you meditate on God's Word.

There are many Scriptures that exhort believers to allow the Holy Spirit to instruct them. You might be thinking, *Well, I'm just not very spiritual. I haven't read through the entire Bible; I don't pray in tongues for two or three hours a day. I don't get excited, dance, or even clap my hands during worship.*

But the Bible doesn't say that you have to do any of that to be led by the Holy Spirit, so don't try to build up some kind of case with requirements that are too hard for you to handle. The bottom line is that if you've been born again, you are the temple of the Holy Spirit. If you are the temple, you've got the Holy Spirit. If you've got the Holy Spirit, you've got the Instructor. If you've got the Instructor; He can do the work of *El Shaddai* (the God who is more than enough) in your situation. It's that easy, so don't try to make things difficult for yourself.

First John 2:20 says, *"But you have an anointing from the Holy One, and you know all things."* The Holy Spirit has given believers a special anointing to know all things. I know—some days, you may not feel so smart, but within you is the *potential* to know all things. I think that's marvelous, especially on the days when I don't feel too swift. It's comforting to know that no matter how tough the situation we are facing, the Holy Spirit will teach us how to Satan-proof our families and keep the devil from doing any damage to our households while we are dealing with the crisis.

Once, when I was on a plane to Atlanta, one of the flight attendants—I'll call her Rachel—told me that she had been born again and was Spirit-filled. She was unsure as to whether she should continue in her profession because she sometimes was required to serve liquor to the airplane passengers. Then, she told me about an incident where a man had become drunk and acted crudely toward the women on the airplane. Rachel had started praying in the Spirit and asked God for a revelation on how to handle this man.

The Holy Spirit had directed her to go and sit next to the intoxicated man. As she sat there and started praying quietly, it wasn't long before the man's hand moved to her leg. Rachel pushed his hand away and said, "I know you have a wonderful wife at home who is praying for you, and you're just living and acting like a dog! What is wrong with you?"

Well, the man was stunned, and asked, "How did you know my wife is a Christian?" Rachel continued to blast him, saying, "You're a lecherous, lustful man, and I'm going to cast those evil spirits out of you right now!" Once she did that, the man was immediately set free, and he gave his life to the Lord right there on that airplane.

Folks, some of you probably won't agree with me, but I don't believe we can put God in a box and tell Him how, where, or when to use people. I am certainly not encouraging Christians to become involved in sinful lifestyles. But I do know that Satan is getting his clutches into one precious soul after another because believers have been content to stay hidden away in their comfortable church buildings instead of doing what God intended—subduing the earth!

Give Spiritual Encouragement

Remember how we talked in the first chapter about Satan-proofing our relationships by praying in the Holy Spirit? If you need a refresher, read Jude 20–21. Now I want to tell you some practical things concerning how you treat your family members so that you'll know exactly what happens when you pray in the Holy Spirit.

I believe that praying in the Spirit gives us a special anointing to love people who may not be entirely lovable at that particular time. Let's be honest—it's not easy to keep loving a spouse who says all kinds of terrible things that cut you to your heart. It's a fact that no one else can hurt you as deeply as your spouse or your children. But, if you want to keep the devil out of those relationships, you'll have to pray in the Holy Spirit, and then God will build you up in those hurting places. God will help you to stay focused on His wonderful love instead of focusing on the offenses, hurts, wounds, and defeats that the devil will try to intensify in your heart.

> *God will help you to stay focused on His wonderful love instead of focusing on the offenses, hurts, wounds, and defeats that the devil will try to intensify in your heart.*

Praying in the Holy Spirit will reveal God's image of your children to you. Sometimes, I think we Christians tend to be too critical of our children—we expect them to be perfect. Folks, our children need our encouragement

47

more than they need anything else from us as parents. We need to let our children know that they are precious and valuable to God, as well as to our family units.

Of course, we are to train up our children in the Word of God; we are to administer proper and consistent correction to them. But we are also to help them to understand that the reason we correct them is that we esteem them highly. Do your children know that they will be better off because you have corrected them? Are they encouraged—built up, edified—after you have corrected them? Or do they just feel worthless and defeated?

The ratio of encouragement to constructive criticism that we give our children should be 90 percent encouragement to 10 percent criticism. Take time to evaluate your interactions with your children and make sure that you are giving out more encouragement than criticism. Then, make sure that the criticism you give is always constructive. If you find yourself deficient in encouragement, begin to increase the amount of time you spend praying in the Holy Spirit. God will give you a revelation of how He sees your children, and He will increase your love for them, even while they are being rebellious.

I know that raising children is difficult, and it's easy to become critical. It's so easy to lose your patience and become fed up with your children; it's so easy to give up and decide not to deal with them. But, let me warn you: if you don't deal with your children, you can bet that the devil will! He just loves to see children who feel neglected, unwanted, or inferior. He has all kinds of bright, glittery enticements to offer them—money, drugs, fast cars, and wrong friendships. There are all kinds of vicious things just waiting to swallow your children up, and they will be lost in a subculture from which, without God, there is little hope of escape.

However, we can keep the devil away from our children by encouraging them, and we can receive a special anointing to do this from God when we pray in the Holy Spirit.

Let's talk about knowledge. *"We know that we all have knowledge. Knowledge puffs up, but love edifies"* (1 Corinthians 8:1). We all can *know* how to treat people. There are thousands of "how-to" books and articles available that will give you step-by-step directions to develop fulfilling relationships with your spouse and children. But it is apparent that this type of knowledge is not working because the "failure of the family" phenomenon continues to sweep through Christian homes. This is because most believers are not Satan-proofing their families by praying. Most of us are not encouraging ourselves in the love of God concerning our families. Instead, we are only gathering knowledge, and knowledge without love elevates believers' pride to a dangerous level. As the apostle Paul wrote, *"Though I...understand all mysteries and all knowledge,...but have not love, I am nothing"* (1 Corinthians 13:2).

Many Christians have elevated themselves so highly in the vast knowledge available on how to construct healthy relationships that they have become mechanical in their thinking. People with this kind of pride don't enjoy other people—they don't enjoy their children, and they certainly don't enjoy their spouses. There is no godly love operating in this mind-set but only an attitude that says, "I'm the expert," or "I always know the correct way to do things." I say, how boring to be with someone who thinks he knows everything all the time! Even if the person was right all the time, I wouldn't want to be around him or her.

As a pastor's wife, I have heard this complaint many times, and I can tell you that your relationships will function so much better if you don't try to be the one who knows everything. And, if you feel like you have to know everything, be sure that the first thing you know about is godly love.

True, godly love is not the emotional feeling that comes over us from time to time. Rather, it's the real action of loving—the *doing* of beneficial things for those with whom we come into contact. You'll discover this kind of love only by spending time praying in the Holy Spirit. Then, you'll be able to take His instructions and Satan-proof your household by encouraging, building up, and edifying your family members in the love of God.

THE HOLY SPIRIT BRINGS LIFE

Another thing you'll need to have in a Satan-proofed home is the life of God operating in your household.

Many Christian homes simply have too much death lurking around. Believers need to bring forth the life of God in their homes by praying in the Holy Spirit.

You may be saying, "What does she mean? There is no death in my house." There are many ways that death can come into your home. One way is through the school systems. If your children attend a public school, you need to be aware that their minds are being filled with death on a daily basis. Of course, they are learning theories, principles, and academic subjects that are necessary for them to function in the world. But, there is so much other dead thinking being forced into their minds—things like evolution, materialism, and how to participate in "safe sex."

Death also can infiltrate your household through an unsaved spouse. Now, I don't want any of you to say, "Marilyn said I should get rid of my unsaved spouse." I didn't say that. The Bible assures us that one believing spouse sanctifies the household. (See 1 Corinthians 7:14.) However, if your spouse is unsaved, he or she is spiritually dead, and you need to counteract that spirit of death with the Spirit of life. That happens when you pray regularly.

There are other things that you need to be vigilant about, such as the music that your children listen to and the movies that they watch. Which television programs does your family watch? Satan is subtle, and he won't always come in with a loud crash. Sometimes, he will slither in quietly like a snake, but he always brings death and destruction.

By contrast, God always has brought life into dead situations through the power of the Holy Spirit.

> *In the beginning God created the heavens and the earth. The earth was without form, and void; and darkness was on the face of the deep. And the Spirit of God was hovering over the face of the waters.* (Genesis 1:1–2)

Before creation, the world was in turmoil, confusion, and havoc. The Spirit of God brooded over the earth and turned chaos (confusion) into cosmos (order). The dictionary defines *cosmos* as "an orderly harmonious systematic universe."

When you start praying in tongues, the Holy Spirit will brood over your household, and He will bring forth life and divine order where before there was death and confusion.

> *"It is the Spirit who gives life; the flesh profits nothing. The words that I speak to you are spirit, and they are life.* (John 6:63)

Try it. Just begin to walk through your house praying in the Spirit. Pray over your couch and over the kitchen chairs. Husbands and wives, pray together over your bed. Pray over each other's clothes and shoes, saying, "Lord, let the person who wears these walk in the life of the Holy Spirit."

I pray over my household all the time. M
is a pastor, and I always pray over his pillow
his clothes. When my daughter, Sarah, was
I would sometimes walk into her room and pray over
her bed, asking God to give her special wisdom. I also
would ask the Holy Spirit to give her life because I
knew how students like to stay up so late. I believe that
God quickened her mind and her body so that she could
comprehend and learn better during the day.

Praying in the Spirit is like a thirsty man taking a
long drink of water. The more you pray in the Spirit, the
thirstier you become, and the thirstier you become, the
more you will pray. It's like a spiral. And there is this
promise from God: *"For I will pour water on him who
is thirsty, and floods on the dry ground; I will pour My
Spirit on your descendants, And My blessing on your
offspring"* (Isaiah 44:3).

The more you drink of the
Holy Spirit, the thirstier you
become, and, because of your
thirst, God will pour His Spirit
out on you and your children.
Then, they, too, will begin to
thirst after the Spirit of the
Lord. There is a connection in
the spirit realm between parents and children. So, if you
want your children to become

> *The more you
> drink of the
> Holy Spirit, the
> thirstier you
> become, and,
> because of your
> thirst, God will
> pour His Spirit
> out on you and
> your children.*

53

spiritual, make sure that you are spiritual, and spend a lot of time in prayer.

TAKING A STAND

In order to Satan-proof our homes, we must take a stand against the devil. This happens when believers become involved in intercessory prayer. *"Put on the whole armor of God, that you may be able to stand against the wiles of the devil"* (Ephesians 6:11).

Wow! This Scripture continues to describe the armor of God:

> *Therefore take up the whole armor of God, that you may be able to withstand in the evil day, and having done all, to stand. Stand therefore, having girded your waist with truth, having put on the breastplate of righteousness, and having shod your feet with the preparation of the gospel of peace; above all, taking the shield of faith with which you will be able to quench all the fiery darts of the wicked one. And take the helmet of salvation, and the sword of the Spirit, which is the word of God; praying always with all prayer and supplication in the Spirit.*
>
> (Ephesians 6:13–18)

It's quite an outfit, isn't it? When you decide to Satan-proof your home through intercessory prayer, you must put on *"the breastplate of righteo* which will make you bolder because you'll be walking in God's righteousness and not your own. *"The helmet of salvation"* will protect your mind from thinking any thoughts that the devil would like you to think. Now, the devil will still bring destructive thoughts to you. He'll tell you that you are a failure, that your spouse doesn't love you, and that your children are the pits. But you don't have to dwell on that kind of junk because your mind is protected by the helmet of salvation!

What does all this armor sound like? It sounds to me as if someone is preparing for battle! These are battle clothes. You say, "But, Marilyn, I'm not going to be out in the mission fields or fighting to further the gospel through evangelism. I'm just going to be in my bedroom praying for my family." Okay, then your bedroom will become a battlefield. That's where you are going to take your stand and tell the devil that he cannot have your marriage, your children, your relatives, your friends, your finances, your future—or anything else that pertains to you!

In Isaiah, it says,

> *When the enemy comes in like a flood, the Spirit of the LORD will lift up a standard against him.*
> (Isaiah 59:19)

The word *standard* here refers to something that causes something else to vanish or flee. James 4:7

says, *"Submit to God. Resist the devil and he will flee from you."*

Once you have clothed yourself in the armor of God, then you, the intercessor, become the standard that God wants to lift up. Through the power of Christ Jesus, God wants you to resist the devil on behalf of your loved ones. And, when you have submitted your life to Christ and have begun to develop a more intimate relationship with Him, the devil will flee from your home when you command him to do so in Jesus' name. God wants you to Satan-proof your family by becoming such a powerful intercessor that the devil won't want to waste his time by stopping at your house!

Chapter Three

Bless Your Household

It's important for you to understand that Satan-proofing your home is not just a "one-shot deal." I say this because some of you will only put into action one of the principles outlined in this book, and you'll think that your home is safe. Then, when the devil interrupts your life again, you'll say, "Hey, Marilyn, it didn't work!" But it's not that the principles don't work; it's that they all work when applied *together* and practiced *regularly*.

Satan-proofing your home is an ongoing process—it's a lifestyle. It's also similar to a puzzle: receiving Christ as your personal Savior is one piece, reading your Bible is another piece, applying the Word of God to your own flesh and to your circumstances is another piece, praying in the Holy Spirit is a piece, and speaking forth God's blessings is yet another piece. If we put all these pieces into their proper places, pretty soon, we'll have a clearer picture of the image in which God created us—His image. And He was the original Satan-proofer!

BLESSINGS AND BENEFITS

I have noticed something special about a Satan-proofed home: it just seems to overflow with wonderful blessings from God. Did you know that God began to bless people immediately after He created them? "*So God created man in His own image; in the image of God He created him; male and female He created them. Then God blessed them*" (Genesis 1:27–28).

The Hebrew word translated here as "*blessed*," *barak*, means "to kneel" (*Strong's* #1288). God put Adam and Eve in a kneeling posture—a position of worship. Why? So that He could begin to prosper them with children and give them control over the earth. Of course, we know that they got out of the posture of worshipping God and into the posture of worshipping their own desires. They really blew it big time—not only for themselves, but for everyone else, as well.

So, we know that God's desire is to bless His people. I don't mean to suggest that God is like Santa Claus and blesses us with "gifts" like good health, prosperity, or peace in our homes. These things are not *gifts*; rather, they are *benefits* that we receive when we keep ourselves in an attitude of worship. They are the results of living a blessed life.

When we begin to apply God's blessings to our loved ones, we are really saying, "God, put my loved ones in a posture of worship so that they can receive the benefits of being in an intimate relationship with You." Isn't that what you really want for your family? Of course it is! So, when you think about Satan-proofing your home, remember that you need to speak abundant blessings upon your loved ones. Also remember that you must be living with an attitude of worship in order to speak blessings. Folks, we simply cannot live sinful lifestyles and expect to remain consecrated in the authority of God. It just doesn't work that way. In order to bless others, we ourselves must first be blessed.

There are five basic promises implied in the verb *bless*: to benefit, to make whole, to prosper, to make healthy, and to make wealthy. When you speak God's blessings, you are reminding Him of His promises. You're saying, "Father, I remind You of Your promises to Your covenant children to benefit us, to make us whole, to prosper us, and to make us healthy and wealthy."

> *The act of blessing is not to be taken lightly, because when we believers mix faith with blessings, we prompt God to move on His promises.*

If you want a Satan-proofed home, then begin to bless your loved ones. The act of blessing is not to be taken lightly, because when we believers mix faith with blessings, we prompt God to move on His promises. So, whatever circumstances you may be facing, begin to bless the people involved.

FOUR AREAS OF BLESSING

There are four areas where God wants His blessings to overflow in the lives of His people: in our circumstances, toward our enemies, toward the Lord, and in our homes.

Wouldn't you like to see God's blessings manifested in all of your circumstances? How about at your workplace? Some of you are experiencing difficulties because your boss favors another employee over you. You have become offended, and you want to jump up and quit. But, have you considered that God may want you to stay there to be a conduit for Him to pour out His blessings upon those people? Hang in there, and thank God for your job. Begin to bless your boss, as well as the other employee; God will bless everyone involved and move on your behalf, as well.

Another area where God wants to manifest His wonderful benefits is toward your enemies. He commands us, *"Love your enemies, bless those who curse you, do good to those who hate you, and pray for those who spitefully use you and persecute you, that you may be sons of your Father in heaven"* (Matthew 5:44–45). You say, "Marilyn, that's where I blow it. I simply cannot bless my enemies."

All right, let's take a closer look at our enemies. We know that our real enemy is the devil. But, in terms of other people, let's define our enemies as those who either knowingly or unknowingly allow themselves to be used by the devil for the purpose of harming us.

I believe most Christians probably would agree that murderers, robbers, rapists, and the like are our enemies. Certainly, these people are dangerous. Yet, many of you may have been injured by parents who have neglected or abused you. Some of you may have spouses who are thoughtless and cruel; perhaps, they have even deserted you. Others of you may have "best friends" who spread your deepest secrets and gossip about you. And still others of you may have been manipulated or hurt by fellow Christians.

There are two things that I want you to see in all these situations. Someone has been injured, and someone has been used as a tool by the devil. I am not making light of the personal suffering that you may have experienced at the hands of another person. But, isn't the person who injured you really just a victim, too? I believe that Satan uses people against each other to carry out his diabolical schemes to steal, to kill, and to destroy God's people. (See John 10:10.)

Think about this the next time someone comes against you, and remember that a Satan-proofer blesses his enemies. Is it easy? No! But it can be done by a believer who lives with an attitude of worship, someone who wants to see God's loving benefits manifested more fully in other people's lives.

God also wants to bless us in our relationships with Him. The psalmist expressed joy at God's blessings, saying,

Bless the LORD, O my soul, and forget not all His benefits: who forgives all your iniquities, who

heals all your diseases, who redeems your life from destruction, who crowns you with loving-kindness and tender mercies, who satisfies your mouth with good things, so that your youth is re-newed like the eagle's. (Psalm 103:2–5)

God is blessed by our obedience, our praise, and our worship. When we bless God, we create an environment in which His blessings can flourish in our lives.

Another area where God wants to bless us is in our homes. Given the choice, most of us would like to see God's benefits flow in our lives and the lives of our loved ones.

> **You can bless your children all through the day, as God's Word is not bound by time or distance.**

You can bless your children all through the day, as God's Word is not bound by time or distance. Speak each child's name and say, "God bless you in your schoolwork." Bless your children especially after they have been disciplined. Go to your child and say, "You have been misbehaving, but I love you, and I am asking God to bless you." I believe that when you mix your faith with the blessing, you'll see an improvement in your child's behavior, attitude, and academic performance.

A woman on my staff has a fifteen-year-old daughter whose rebellious behavior was adversely affecting her performance in school. The woman prayed and sought God's wisdom for the situation. Then, she began to speak God's blessings into her daughter's life. As the mother became more aware of the need to speak words of encouragement rather than criticism, her daughter's attitude and academic performance began to improve.

We wives who want to Satan-proof our homes need to bless our husbands, even when they're grumpy or mean. If your husband hurts you with unkind words or actions, resist the urge to retaliate or pout. Instead, pray in private and speak God's blessings upon him. It's not easy, I know, and some of you may be thinking, *Marilyn, I can't bless my husband—I'd rather strangle him!* Nevertheless, you must bless him—even if you have to say, "God, I'm angry with my husband right now, but by faith, I ask You to bless him."

THE PRIESTHOOD AND BLESSINGS

Now let's look at what actually happens when we speak God's blessings. The Bible says that God instructed the priests to bless the children of Israel:

And the LORD spoke to Moses, saying: "Speak to Aaron and his sons, saying, 'This is the way you shall bless the children of Israel. Say to them: "The LORD bless you and keep you; the LORD make His face shine upon you, and be gracious to you; the LORD lift up His countenance upon you, and give you peace." So they shall put My name on the children of Israel, and I will bless them."' (Numbers 6:22–27)

What happened when the Israelites were blessed?

And Moses and Aaron went into the tabernacle of meeting, and came out and blessed the people. Then the glory of the LORD appeared to all the people. (Leviticus 9:23)

When the priests blessed the people, God's glory appeared. Blessings bring forth a manifestation of the glory of God. You may be thinking, *That was fine for ancient Israel, but where are the modern-day priests?*

The Bible says that believers are kings and priests:

And from Jesus Christ,...To Him who loved us and washed us from our sins in His own blood, and has made us kings and priests to His God and Father. (Revelation 1:5–6)

Do you want to see God's glory manifested in your family, your place of employment, your church, your nation, and the world? Then you must exercise the authority given to you by Christ Jesus. You must begin to function as a priest to the people with whom you have contact and start speaking God's blessings into their lives.

I pray and speak God's blessings over my family, ministry, and ministry partners, over the United States, and over the world. Folks, if we want to see God manifest His glory, then we have to stop whining about how bad things are, take our priestly positions, and begin to Satan-proof the world!

The Bible clearly explains the major duties of priests:

At that time the LORD separated the tribe of Levi to bear the ark of the covenant of the LORD, to stand before the LORD to minister to Him and to bless in His name, to this day.

(Deuteronomy 10:8)

What was so important about the ark of the covenant? It contained the Ten Commandments (the way), the golden pot of manna (the truth), and Aaron's rod that budded (the life). The way, the truth, and the life—who is that? Jesus, of course! (See John 14:6.) The Old Testament priests carried the ark of the covenant, and the things it contained were pictures of the real thing—Jesus!

The Bible also says that the priests ministered to God. This means that they lived their lives with an attitude of worship. They absolutely could not be in God's presence without being consecrated. And then, they blessed people *in His name.*

But you are a chosen generation, a royal priesthood, a holy nation, His own special people, that you may proclaim the praises of Him who called you out of darkness into His marvelous light.

(1 Peter 2:9)

That's us. Christians are now God's believer-priests. What does God want His priests—believers—to do today? He wants us to take the love and authority of Jesus Christ to the world. God wants us to live with an *attitude of worship* and to bless people in the name of Jesus.

One of the many benefits that God wants His people to receive is forgiveness. In order for the Israelites to receive forgiveness for their sins, the Old Testament priests had to offer blood sacrifices. I would have thought, *What a pain to have to kill an animal every time we blow it.* I am so glad that we have the new covenant, which was established through the shed blood of Jesus Christ. We don't have to make any more sacrifices because one drop of Christ's sinless blood was enough to atone for all the sins in the world.

> **We don't have to make any more sacrifices because one drop of Christ's sinless blood was enough to atone for all the sins in the world.**

There's something else worth noting about blessings. In Deuteronomy 33:1, we see that Moses blessed the children of Israel before his death. Moses went on to prophesy over all of the tribes of Israel. The word *bless* is defined as "to confer prosperity or happiness upon." What was Moses doing? He was conferring prosperity and happiness upon the Israelites.

What about those of you who are fathers? Do you confer prosperity and happiness upon your children? Do you declare that they are going to do well in school and in their relationships? Do you declare them to be winners in every situation that they encounter? If you want to stop the devil from luring your kids away from the Lord, then you need to begin to bless them. Don't forget that a child who feels like a worthless loser is vulnerable to Satan's deceptions.

BLESS YOUR CIRCUMSTANCES

Have you ever known someone whose life and circumstances were obviously being flooded with God's glory, but he didn't even know it? A man named Balak, the king of Moab, experienced this very thing.

The Bible tells us how Balak was nervous when the Israelites were passing through Moab on their way to the Promised Land. When Balak heard that they were camped in Moab, he became terrified. He had heard about how the Israelites had killed two Amorite kings, Sihon and Og, and had taken a huge land giant. (See Numbers 21:33–35; 22:1–3.)

Picture the Israelites. They were ex-slaves who had been in bondage for over four hundred years, and they were totally untrained in warfare. Yet, they had succeeded in conquering a land that no one else had been able to conquer. It was obvious to everyone else that they'd had supernatural help from God. People were saying to one another, "Did you hear what happened? Those Israelites got all that land when they overcame Sihon and Og. They did it because they worship some kind of God who blesses them!"

This was also frightening to the Perizzites, the Hivites, and the rest of those "-ites." They all panicked when they heard that the Israelites were coming. After all, Israel had a mighty God who had parted the Red Sea and had killed all those Egyptians, including Pharaoh! Then, Israel's God had helped them kill Sihon and Og, two more kings.

So, when Balak heard that the Israelites were in his country, he naturally wondered, *Am I going to be the next to die?* Poor Balak didn't realize that he and his people were blessed because God had commanded the Israelites not to harm them. Why? Because the Moabites were descendants of Abraham's nephew, Lot, which made them shirttail relatives of the Israelites, who were direct descendants of Abraham.

Remember when Lot and his two daughters escaped the judgment on Sodom and went to live in a cave in the mountains? Well, Lot's daughters got him drunk and committed incest with him. The oldest daughter named her son Moab, and he became the father of the Moabites. (See Genesis 19:30–37.)

Despite the Moabites' bad beginning, God had blessed them and had told the Israelites not to harm them. But since Balak didn't know God and had no clue that the Israelites wouldn't harm the Moabites, he hired the prophet Balaam to curse Israel. Balaam tried and tried to curse the Israelites. He even climbed two different mountains and tried to curse them, but every time he opened his mouth, only blessings came forth. (See Numbers 22:5–23:11.)

Finally, he told Balak,

Behold, I have received a command to bless; He has blessed, and I cannot reverse it.

(Numbers 23:20)

Balaam was saying, in effect, "I cannot curse these people because they have God's blessings upon them, and what God has blessed, no one can curse." What a startling revelation! And, folks, the same thing is true today. When you begin to Satan-proof your relationships and circumstances by speaking forth the blessings of God, you can believe that no devilish curse will come against them!

> *When you begin to Satan-proof your relationships and circumstances by speaking forth the blessings of God, you can believe that no devilish curse will come against them!*

Speak Blessings, Not Curses

Let me show you something about how marital strife and problems with our children are affected by the words we speak. You may say, "I'm a Christian, so I never speak curses upon other people." But what about the hateful, negative things we say to one another?

What happens when some husbands come home from work? They look at their wives and say, "Why do you wear that old thing? You are so fat. When are you going to go on a diet!"

Or, sometimes wives may look at their husbands and say, "You have bad breath and you smell. Go brush your teeth and take a shower!"

And some of us aren't any better with our children. We may say, "You'll never amount to anything! How did you get so stupid? You look horrible!"

Are we blessing, or are we cursing? If you want the devil to steal your marriage, just continue talking to your spouse in a negative manner. As far as your sons and daughters are concerned, I already told you that the devil is on the prowl for children with poor self-esteem. And where do you think your child's sense of self-esteem is developed? In the home, of course.

I know of a young couple who were having some marital problems. Once, when they were preparing to celebrate a particular holiday, the wife gave her husband an ultimatum: he would have to do things her way or pack his things and get out!

The husband quickly recognized that the devil was trying to destroy his marriage. So, instead of becoming angry, this young believer got out his blessing oil and began to anoint his home—the doors, the windows, the dresser drawers, the driveway, and so forth. This husband began to speak blessings on his wife and into their marriage. Today, that couple is still together, and their marriage continues to grow in the Lord.

That young man had a choice, didn't he? He could have just thrown the doors to his marriage wide open and let Satan rob him blind. Instead, he Satan-proofed his household and spoke blessings upon his circumstances.

Blessings are on the head of the righteous, but violence covers the mouth of the wicked.
(Proverbs 10:6)

Let me tell you about someone else who blessed his circumstances: Joseph.

So Esau hated Jacob because of the blessing with which his father blessed him, and Esau said in his heart, "The days of mourning for my father are at hand; then I will kill my brother Jacob."
(Genesis 27:41)

I would say that someone hating his brother enough to want to kill him is pretty serious, wouldn't you? Why did Esau hate Jacob? Because Jacob had received the firstborn blessing from their father, Isaac. As the oldest son, Esau was supposed to inherit the blessing, but he had become careless about spiritual things and had sold his birthright to Jacob for a bowl of stew. (See Genesis 25:30–34.) However, Esau was not the only one in the

71

wrong; Jacob used a lot of trickery to get the blessing. Esau got so mad at Jacob that he threatened to kill him, but he never did. Why? Because God's blessings were upon Jacob, and what God had blessed could not be cursed.

When Rebekah found out that her son Esau wanted to kill his brother, she sent Jacob to live with her brother, Laban. Before Jacob left home, his father Isaac blessed him again.

> *May God Almighty bless you, and make you fruitful and multiply you, that you may be an assembly of peoples; and give you the blessing of Abraham, to you and your descendants with you, that you may inherit the land in which you are a stranger, which God gave to Abraham.*
>
> (Genesis 28:3–4)

The Bible tells us that Jacob certainly prospered during the fourteen years that he lived in Haran with his uncle. Jacob married two of Laban's daughters, Leah and Rachel, and fathered twelve sons. Jacob also became wealthy:

> *Thus the man became exceedingly prosperous, and had large flocks, female and male servants, and camels and donkeys.* (Genesis 30:43)

Eventually, Jacob returned from Haran to Canaan, and it's interesting to see how he treated Esau. Jacob knew that he could not avoid meeting Esau—I don't think Jacob was looking forward to seeing his brother at all. He knew that he had taken unfair advantage of Esau, and that he had good reason to be afraid of him.

So, Jacob had an all-night prayer meeting, and God dealt with him about his own attitude. When Jacob finally did encounter Esau, he didn't reopen the old wound. Instead, Jacob blessed Esau with gifts and allowed God to defuse that potentially explosive situation. (See Genesis 33:1–11.)

Folks, there is a simple truth working here that we need to grasp. Speaking God's blessings over our circumstances will bring forth life and God's benefits, and speaking curses over our circumstances will bring forth death.

Speak Positive Words, Not Negative Ones

There was another man who really understood the importance of speaking forth blessings—David.

Then David returned to bless his household. And Michal the daughter of Saul came out to meet David. (2 Samuel 6:20)

David had returned from Kirjath-jearim, where he had gone to bring the ark of the covenant to Jerusalem. This was a blessed occasion, and there was a tremendous praise and worship service going on. David was leaping and dancing before the Lord with all his might. He went to bless his household, and his wife, Michal, came out to meet him. Did she graciously receive God's blessings spoken by her husband? No. Instead, she said,

> *How glorious was the king of Israel today, uncovering himself today in the eyes of the maids of his servants, as one of the base fellows shamelessly uncovers himself!*   (2 Samuel 6:20)

Michal could have added her blessings to an already blessed occasion, but she did not. Instead, Michal spoke negatively to her husband and dishonored him.

Are you like Michal? Are their times when your spouse or your child has been in a great mood and rushed in to share his joy with you, only to have you snap at him or bite off his head with negative words?

That's what Michal did, and her negative words had the effect of a curse on her own life. She never was able to have children for the rest of her life. (See 2 Samuel 6:23.) On the other hand, from David's descendants came Jesus. David's blessings were eternal.

I believe that some of you wives might feel sorry for Michal and say, "Well, she didn't like the way David was acting, dancing half-naked in the street. She had a right to speak negatively." Let me share with you a woman's testimony about how negative words almost ended her twenty-year marriage.

Carol had been standing in faith for her husband and son, who were members of a cult. Carol herself had been delivered from the cult just months before. Now, Carol could have become really negative with her husband—after all, she had been born again; she had the truth. She could have been very harsh and said, "Get out of there, because, if you don't, you're going to hell!"

But negative words could have ended her marriage. So, Carol didn't speak negative, critical words. Instead, she studied the Bible and began to bless her marriage. She prayed for her family and began to thank God regularly for her husband. Less than a year later, both her husband and son came to the Lord, left the cult, and were filled with the Spirit.

When we Satan-proof our circumstances by speaking forth God's blessings, we reap blessings. But speaking forth negative words brings only a curse. God wants us to bless one another's circumstances like Joshua blessed Caleb: *"And Joshua blessed him, and gave Hebron to Caleb the son of Jephunneh as an inheritance"* (Joshua 14:13).

> **When we Satan-proof our circumstances by speaking forth God's blessings, we reap blessings.**

Joshua had led the Israelites into the Promised Land, and now he was getting the people situated into the areas where they were supposed to settle. Caleb had said, "Joshua, I want that piece of land that I claimed when we first came to Canaan as spies." So, Joshua blessed Caleb and gave him the land he desired.

When we follow Caleb's life, we see that he was one of the most blessed men of God. And Caleb blessed his daughter, Achsah, even after she married and left his care. She ended up marrying a Spirit-filled man

75

named Othniel, who later became the first judge in Israel.

I think Caleb was a wise father. Sadly, many parents today want to get their children out of their homes quickly and therefore aren't too concerned about the people with whom their children become involved. But Caleb made the announcement that whoever wanted to marry Achsah would first have to kill some giants and take their land. (See Joshua 15:16.) This may sound like an impossible challenge, but during that time, there were giants living in the land. Caleb had killed a few of them, and he wanted to be sure that his daughter's husband could protect her from every type of enemy.

By requiring that his future son-in-law be a killer of giants, Caleb gave Achsah the assurance that her husband would not be lazy—lazy men do not fight giants. Also, she would be assured that her husband would be absolutely wild about her, for only the man who sincerely loved her would be willing to risk his life to marry her.

Achsah probably wished her father hadn't issued that challenge. I am certain that her chances of finding a husband who would kill a giant looked very slim. But, then, Othniel, whose name means "Force of God," showed up, and he certainly lived up to his name.

You see, Caleb was blessed by God and by men. He wisely blessed the future circumstances of Achsah's life by making it impossible for just anyone to marry her. I cannot emphasize this enough: parents need to bless their children in every way. They also need to bless their children's future mates before they ever meet.

The last model I want to point out to you about blessing one another's circumstances is Ruth, who was a Moabitess. Ruth had been brought up in idolatry. The Moabites worshipped an idol called *Chemosh*, which means "a dunghill deity." Idolatry also carries a curse, and so Ruth was in trouble! This curse was reversed when Ruth turned to God. When she renounced Chemosh, the curse was broken completely, and tremendous blessings came upon Ruth.

After Ruth's husband died, she decided to return to Bethlehem with her mother-in-law, Naomi, instead of staying in Moab with her own family. She said to Naomi,

Entreat me not to leave you, Or to turn back from following after you; for wherever you go, I will go; and wherever you lodge, I will lodge; your people shall be my people, and your God, my God.
(Ruth 1:16)

When they arrived in Bethlehem, Ruth went to work gleaning in the field of Naomi's wealthy relative, Boaz. She followed Naomi's advice, and, very soon, Boaz wanted to marry Ruth. He went to the elders of the city and fulfilled the tedious legal procedures involved with marrying. There were a lot of logistics that had to be worked out, but Boaz finally got everything straightened out, and he and Ruth were married. (See Ruth 4:1–13.)

Look at the blessings that the elders spoke into Boaz and Ruth's marriage:

> *The L*ORD *make the woman who is coming to your house like Rachel and Leah, the two who built the house of Israel....May your house be like the house of Perez, whom Tamar bore to Judah, because of the offspring which the L*ORD *will give you from this young woman.*   (Ruth 4:11–12)

This ceremony was not only about a man taking a wife. More important, the elders also were blessing the circumstances of Boaz and Ruth's life together. The elders prayed for Ruth to be like Rachel and Leah, Jacob's wives, who had borne the children who had become the heads of the twelve tribes of Israel. The elders also prayed for Ruth to be like Judah's daughter-in-law, Tamar, who had borne twin sons, Perez and Zerah. (See Genesis 38:11–30.) The children of these three women had been blessed, and the elders were speaking the same blessings upon Ruth. But, could Ruth's offspring be such a blessing? After all, Rachel, Leah, and Tamar were Israelites, while Ruth was a Moabitess.

You see, the Israelites knew the prophecy recorded in Genesis 3:15: "*And I will put enmity between you and the woman, and between your seed and her Seed; He shall bruise your head, and you shall bruise His heel.*" This was a Messianic prophecy, and all of the Israelite women wanted to bring forth the seed about which it spoke. However, the Messiah would come only through the lineage of Judah: *"The scepter shall not depart from Judah, nor a lawgiver from between his feet, until Shiloh comes; and to Him shall be the obedience of the people"* (Genesis 49:10).

The Bible records five women in the genealogy of Jesus Christ, and Ruth is among these women. (See Matthew 1:5.) Do you wonder how she got there? Well, Boaz was from the tribe of Judah, and he and Ruth had a son named Obed. Obed's son was Jesse, and Jesse was the father of David. Ruth was David's great-grandmother, so she wound up in the genealogy of Jesus Christ!

God's blessings are absolutely powerful, and I pray that you will become a Satan-proofer and begin to function as a priest to the people closest to you. As you speak forth God's wonderful blessings, people will come into an *attitude of worship* and begin to walk in the tremendous benefits that accompany the manifestation of God's glory!

Chapter Four

Come Out of the Closet

Have you noticed lately that all kinds of people are "coming out of the closet" and demanding that the whole world acknowledge who they are and what they are doing? Regardless of the lifestyle in which they may be involved, these people want to be noticed. They want their lifestyles to be accepted as "normal."

God wants His people to set a strong example for what is the normal lifestyle—we Christians should be the ones who are most noticed. I travel all over the world, and I have become concerned by the number of Christians who seem to be confused about what is involved in living a truly Christian lifestyle.

Many of us are quick to say that we are following Christ's example, but do you know that wherever Jesus went, He caused a stir? His lifestyle included preaching the gospel, healing the sick, feeding the poor, and getting people delivered from the devil. Folks, you can't lead that kind of lifestyle without stirring up something!

You say, "Well, that refers to people in leadership positions. I'm not called to go out and minister to large crowds of people." Maybe you're not, but aren't we Christians supposed to minister to the people with whom we come in contact—like family members, friends, co-workers, hairstylists, or gas station attendants? Let me ask you, Does the cashier at your favorite grocery store know you are a Christian? What about your neighbors? Or your doctor? Or even your in-laws?

Is the fact that you have been born again and baptized in the power of the Holy Spirit making a difference in the life of someone other than you? If not, then you need to "come out of the closet" so that Jesus can use you to do His Father's work here on earth.

When I say "come out of the closet," I am referring to coming out of the complacent mind-set held by so many believers today. *Complacency* means "self-satisfaction especially when accompanied by unawareness of actual dangers or deficiencies." Many people are self-satisfied because they attend church regularly; don't drink, smoke, or commit adultery—and think they are imitating Christ. But living a clean lifestyle alone does not reflect Christ. Of course, Jesus lived a clean life; however, He also preached the gospel, healed the sick, fed the hungry, and delivered people from the clutches of Satan. Ask yourself, *Am I really imitating Christ, or have I become complacent in a lifestyle that has little effect on anyone other than myself?*

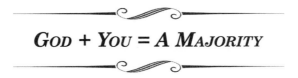

GOD + YOU = A MAJORITY

Being victorious in spiritual warfare means knowing you can do all things through Christ, who strengthens you. (See Philippians 4:13.) It means coming out of the closet and taking charge of your circumstances. Satan-proofers bring about change when, by faith, they step out of the comfort zone of familiarity and begin to apply God's Word to the world around them—beginning in their own lives. Applying God's Word to your environment will bring a change—maybe not always a pleasant change, but always a necessary change. These changes will bring your environment into order according to biblical principles.

Change isn't easy because many Christians would rather *lean on* someone than *be leaned on*. They would rather *be prayed for* than *pray for someone else*. It's easier for some of us to blend into the background like chameleons rather than to do what God has called all believers to do: subdue the earth.

Remember, to *subdue* means "to conquer and bring into subjection; vanquish." You may be thinking, *The earth is so big, and there are so many different people with so many different situations. How does God expect us to have an effect on so many different lives?* It's easy— you do it one person at a time. You begin by extending God's love to your family and friends. Pretty soon, you'll be praying and blessing your coworkers, your hairstylist, your gas station attendant—and don't forget the cashier at the grocery store.

When every believer begins to Satan-proof the small part of the earth over which he or she has influence, then the whole earth will be subdued! Won't that

> **When every believer begins to Satan-proof the small part of the earth over which he or she has influence, then the whole earth will be subdued!**

be marvelous? But it won't happen until believers courageously come out of the closet, take a stand, and Satan-proof God's beautiful earth.

As you begin to emerge from the closet, don't be discouraged when the devil starts telling you that you can't win, or that you are all alone. The devil is a liar—don't listen to him! The Bible says that Jesus is always with you, and that you can do all things through Christ, who strengthens you. (See Matthew 28:20; Philippians 4:13.) You can succeed in Satan-proofing your environment because Jesus is with you, and God plus you always equals the majority.

HIDING YOUR CHRISTIAN IDENTITY

Let's look at the life of a young woman named Esther who took charge of her circumstances and literally changed the world. Her situation was very serious, and her actions could have cost her her life; but Esther came out of the closet and saved the people of Israel.

The events recorded in the book of Esther took place while the Israelites were being held in Babylonian captivity. The story begins with Persia's King Ahasuerus throwing a party that lasted six months—it was an extravagant occasion. Ahasuerus spared no expense wining and dining the leaders of the 127 provinces of the Persian Empire. And, since it was not customary for men and women to feast together, Queen Vashti was busily entertaining the wives of these leaders in another part of the palace.

Jewish tradition says that Ahasuerus apparently became overcome by wine because he demanded that his wife come in and display herself to his guests! You know, every time I read this, I say to myself, *What a jerk!* I'm not involved in the women's liberation movement, but I certainly believe that Vashti acted in good taste when she refused her husband's demand.

However, Vashti's refusal presented quite a problem for Ahasuerus. His seven counselors immediately began to warn him that he had better do something about his "rebellious" wife before all the women in the empire followed Vashti's example and rebelled against their husbands. One counselor, Memucan, went so far as to advise the king to divorce Vashti and choose another queen more befitting the position. (See Esther 1:19.) Despite the fact that Ahasuerus may have loved Vashti, to save face, he divorced her. Ahasuerus may have been king over the most powerful empire of that day, but he allowed himself to lose his wife because of his own pride and the unwise counsel of his advisers.

You're probably thinking, *I never would be that stupid!* Hopefully not. But, what about the times when you blew it with your spouse? Did you quickly apologize and make up? Or did you let your "little" mistake escalate into a full-blown incident? Did you call a friend for advice? Did your friend give you godly advice that would bring about reconciliation with your spouse? Or did you call someone whom you knew would sympathize and take sides with you?

I know a woman who was once unhappily married. Her husband abused her physically, drank a great deal, and was neither loving or understanding. Soon, this woman became involved with another man. It was a bad situation, and there was no question of her guilt.

We prayed with this woman and gave her godly counsel to humble herself before the Lord, as well as before her husband. She broke off her relationship with the other man and then humbled herself before her husband, saying, "I have done wrong, and I do not deserve to be your wife." In no way did the woman blame her husband for anything! She humbled *herself.*

However, her husband would not accept her apology, and he divorced her. But, one year later, God had done a work in the husband's life. My husband had the privilege of remarrying them, and they are married to this day!

We counseled this wife according to God's Word to submit and humble herself before her husband. (See 1 Peter 3:1.) I'm sure that it wasn't easy to humble herself, but she received and acted on our godly counsel, and God mercifully intervened and saved her marriage.

The devil does not care how he gets into your relationships—his only goal is to infiltrate them and cause trouble. Satan doesn't have any problem using your pride to destroy your relationships. If you are going to Satan-proof your home, it's important that you never allow pride to hinder you from reconciling with your loved ones. *Come out of the closet!* Come out of your comfort zone. Don't wait for things to "blow over," Bring your circumstances in line with the Word of God!

> *The devil does not care how he gets into your relationships—his only goal is to infiltrate them and cause trouble.*

Even though King Ahasuerus certainly did everything wrong concerning the situation with Queen Vashti, God did get the glory out of the next queen of Persia. After Ahasuerus and Vashti divorced, the king's servants decided to have a beauty contest to choose the next queen. *"Then the king's servants who attended him said: 'Let beautiful young virgins be sought for the king'"* (Esther 2:2).

King Ahasuerus appointed officers to go to all 127 provinces of his kingdom and bring back the most gorgeous women in the empire. Among those women was a lovely young Jewish girl named Hadassah, which means "myrtle tree." Of course, no one knew she was Jewish because she was known by the name Esther, which means "a star." Esther's parents were dead, and she lived with her cousin, Mordecai. (See Esther 2:7.) With Mordecai's help, Esther had been living among the Persian people "in the closet," with her Jewish heritage carefully hidden.

I can think of occasions when it might be "convenient" to let our Christian values slide. For instance, consider the single mother who is concerned that the posters on her teenage son's bedroom walls are somewhat seductive. This mother knows that her son tends to be rebellious and that he gets angry easily. Should this mother insist that her son remove the posters, or should she simply "leave well enough alone" and thank God that at least her son is not doing drugs or in a street gang?

If this mother wants to Satan-proof her teenager, then she has to enforce godly principles in her home. She cannot leave well enough alone. She has to come out of the closet and create a stir in her son's life.

Let's relate this to Esther, who did not reveal her Jewish heritage and went on to win the beauty contest. *"Now the young woman pleased him* [Hegai, the keeper of the king's women], *and she obtained his favor; so he readily gave beauty preparations to her, besides her allowance"* (Esther 2:9).

How many of you Christian husbands get upset when your wives spend too much time in the beauty parlor? It may take your wife three or four hours, but it took Esther a whole year to be prepared to meet the king. Imgaine, soaking in exquisite perfumes and exotic bath oils for one solid year! Sometimes when I come home from getting my hair done, my husband, Wally, will tease me, saying, "Oh, I guess they weren't able to take you today, Marilyn." Despite his attempt at humor, I know Wally appreciates the fact that I take care of myself.

It's sad to say, but many women think that the beautification process stops once the wedding is over. The truth is, that's when it all begins. I know—sometimes, it takes more effort than we may want to put forth, but we women have to come out of our closets of complacency and extend that extra effort. I believe that taking care of your physical appearance and hygiene is a part of Satan–proofing your marriage. Believe me—if you don't care how you look or smell, before long, you will put your husband in a vulnerable position where he could be tempted by the devil to stray from your marriage.

Esther spent one year preparing to go before the king, and she had favor with everyone who looked upon her. (See Esther 1:15.) Do you know that God can give you favor with unsaved people?

I want to encourage you young people—you may think that nobody will like you if you are a Christian. But, if you are true to God, He will give you favor and make you a person of influence in your school. God will use you as a vessel to bless other people. First, you have to come out of the closet and let other people know that you love Jesus, and then God will bless you.

Four years after the big 180-day feast at which Queen Vashti rebelled, Esther finally was taken before Ahasuerus, and she must have been a real knockout.

The king loved Esther more than all the other women, and she obtained grace and favor in his sight more than all the virgins; so he set the royal crown upon her head and made her queen instead of Vashti. (Esther 2:17)

Ahasuerus married Esther, and this young Jewish girl became his queen. Sometimes, when I read the book of Esther, I wonder about Mordecai. After all, he was encouraging Esther to remain "in the closet" and hide the fact that she was one of God's chosen people. Even after Esther married Ahasuerus, Mordecai told her to remain hidden. (See Esther 2:20.) Little did they know that they would be God's provident instruments in a big crisis that was just over the horizon.

Be a Star Shining in the Darkness

I really enjoy studying about the providence of God. It's wonderful to know that we believers are still God's provision for the people in the world, despite the fact that we sometimes fail Him. There are so many times when we allow the pressures of life to hinder us from carrying God's light into a situation.

Years ago, one of our faithful volunteers decided she would surprise me by painting one of the Sunday school rooms at our church. She picked out the color, and she and her son painted the room. When my husband took me into the room, I looked at the walls and said, "Oh, what a terrible color!" I didn't know that the woman and her son were hiding in the closet. Of course, this precious lady was devastated! She ran out of the church, and I ran out behind her, apologizing and asking her to forgive me. When she got into her car, I stuck my head in the window to tell her how sorry I was, but she just rolled up the window and drove off.

Wouldn't you say that, as a pastor's wife, I had blown it? You're right—I had. So, I went home and prayed about it, and I believe that the Lord quickened Colossians 1:20 in my spirit:

> And by [Jesus] to reconcile all things to Himself, by Him, whether things on earth or things in heaven, having made peace through the blood of His cross.

I repented of my actions, applied the blood of Jesus to the situation, and asked God to reconcile me to this woman I had hurt. Before the night was over, she called me and said, "Marilyn, I can't be angry with you. My father is ill, and I need you to pray with me."

Let's face it—we just can't do everything right all the time! That's why it is so encouraging to know that

> *It is so encouraging to know that even when we blow it, God can still use us like stars to reflect the light of Jesus Christ and to dispel the darkness that is attempting to cover the earth.*

even when we blow it, God can still use us like stars to reflect the light of Jesus Christ and to dispel the darkness that is attempting to cover the earth.

Has there ever been a time in your life when you have failed to reflect the light of Christ, perhaps in a witnessing situation? Some of you may think that witnessing is the hardest thing in the world to do. You say, "Oh, I'm just too embarrassed to talk to strangers," or "Everyone has to find his own way; I am not going to force my religious beliefs upon anyone."

Baloney! Do you think this way? Then you need to come out of the closet if you want to be a Satan-proofer. Maybe you won't witness like the next person does, but believers are to be witnesses of God's power in the earth. As you continue to spend time praying and developing your relationship with our wonderful heavenly Father, I believe God will help you to understand better what He wants you to do. God will help you to come out of your closet, and He will use you to reflect the love of Christ—whether you think you're doing it right or not.

It's interesting to see how God brought Esther out of her closet and used her to light up a dark situation. God certainly got a lot of mileage out of Esther's position as Queen of Persia because her relationship to the king saved the Israelites from certain destruction.

Then, something very interesting happened to Mordecai:

While Mordecai sat within the king's gate, two of the king's eunuchs, Bigthan and Teresh, doorkeepers, became furious and sought to lay hands on King Ahasuerus. (Esther 2:21)

Mordecai had overheard these men plotting to assassinate the king! He quickly sent word to Esther, the two would-be assassins were caught and hanged, and Ahasuerus's life was saved. Unfortunately, the king didn't know that it was Mordecai who had saved his life. The Bible says only that *"it was written in the book of the chronicles in the presence of the king"* (verse 23). No gratitude had been extended to Mordecai for his loyalty. Only much later, when the king reviewed the historical chronicles, did he discover what Mordecai had done for him. Do you sometimes feel that no one notices the good things you do?

I believe that many young people often feel that no one ever notices the good things they do. As parents, we are often quick to point out their mistakes, but do we give out as much praise for their accomplishments? They often are confronted with peer pressure in school. They are under a level of temptation that we may never have experienced, and they're trying so hard to stay true to God. Then, when it comes time to get a date for the prom, Christian teens often aren't asked. Why? Because holding true to God's principles has made them unpopular, and being popular is extremely important to a teenager—especially if she expects to be asked to the prom.

We need to encourage young people and acknowledge it when they overcome an obstacle, study extra hard for a subject they hate, say no to drugs, or refuse to participate in "safe sex." As parents, we must be careful about how we relate to our children. Whether we like it or not, they will follow our example when deciding whether to come out of the closet and share their faith with their peers.

Refuse to Compromise

About five years after Esther had been crowned queen, the king promoted Haman to the position of grand vizier. As Ahasuerus's right-hand man, Haman was very prideful and had a burning passion to be exalted above everyone else. Because of his high position in the Persian Empire, Haman was revered, and people bowed down to him—everyone except Mordecai. (See Esther 5:9.)

Although the king's servants repeatedly warned Mordecai about not bowing to Haman, Mordecai would not compromise. Instead, he held his ground and refused to reverence Haman.

Mordecai was not being rebellious; he was obeying the Jewish teaching that forbade him to bow down and worship a man. Also, I believe Mordecai probably knew that Haman was a descendant of the Amalekites, who were ancient enemies of the Israelites and were considered to be cursed. (See Deuteronomy 25:19.)

At any rate, Mordecai would not bow, and Haman was furious! He knew that Mordecai was Jewish, and he hated the Jews because the Israelites had defeated his ancestors, the Amalekites, in a war under the leadership of Moses. So, Haman not only wanted to get his hands on Mordecai, but he also wanted to set into motion a diabolical plan to destroy all the Jews in the Persian Empire.

Doesn't that sound like something the devil would do? Not all the Jews had offended Haman; only Mordecai had done that. We Christians have been known to make mountains out of molehills when we take offense. Many times, we allow a tiny, insignificant offense to grow until it gets blown so far out of proportion that it becomes difficult to bring things back into perspective.

Have you ever found yourself in a similar situation? I have. But I have learned that when I deal with other people's problems according to the Bible, God enlightens the situation and brings it back into line with His Word every time.

When I deal with other people's problems according to the Bible, God enlightens the situation and brings it back into line with His Word every time.

By contrast, Haman used treachery and slander to coax King Ahasuerus into signing an order "*to destroy, to kill, and to annihilate*" (Esther 3:13) all Jews in the 127 provinces of the Persian Empire. In my opinion, Ahasuerus's leadership qualities were the absolute pits! First, he let himself become so intoxicated that he demanded of his wife to degrade herself in front of a bunch of drunken men. Next, he followed the terrible advice of his counselors to divorce Vashti because she refused to obey him. Then, the king chose his new wife, Esther, through a beauty contest. And, now, we see this so-called great king letting himself be manipulated into signing an irreversible document that would create an "open season" for the killing of God's people!

The Bible says that after the devilish decree ordering the murder of the Jewish people went out, the king and Haman sat down to have a drink. But the people of Shushan were perplexed because the Persians had no particular hatred for the Jewish people. For their king to have issued this decree seemed quite out of the ordinary. (See Esther 3:15.)

I believe that is exactly what the devil does to our circumstances. Many times, when we are experiencing a crisis, it may be that the devil is influencing the thinking or actions of the people involved. But, as Satan-proofers, we have made the choice to come out of our closets and allow the light of God to shine brightly in every potentially dark situation.

Let's look at how Mordecai and Esther came out of the closet of complacency and began to counteract the sentence pronounced against the Jewish people. When Mordecai found out what Haman had done, he tore his clothes and began to cry loudly and bitterly in the middle of the city. Also, a great cry went up in every province that received the king's decree. The Jewish people began to fast and to cry out to God. Finally, Esther's attendants told her what had happened. She confirmed it with Mordecai, and Mordecai told Esther that she needed to go to the king and intercede on behalf of the Jewish people. (See Esther 4:1–8.)

After all those years of hiding in the closet of complacency, Esther would have to "rock the boat" and take a stand for her people. This presented a serious problem because it was not customary for the queen to go and see the king without first being summoned. Esther hadn't been summoned by her husband for a month, and if she just barged into the inner court, the king could have killed her. (See Esther 4:11.) Naturally, Esther was hesitant. But Mordecai told her, *"Do not think in your heart that you will escape in the king's palace any more than all the other Jews"* (Esther 4:13). In other words, Mordecai was merely reminding Esther that if all the Jews were killed, she would be killed, too. Perhaps Esther had become so comfortable living a lie that she'd actually forgotten that she, too, was Jewish!

That's not difficult to understand. I believe that many Christians deny or have forgotten that they are Christ's hands extended in the earth. When Christ was physically on earth, He preached the gospel, healed the sick, fed the poor, and delivered people from the devil. God wants believers to do the same—first in our own homes, then in our communities, and then in the world.

Listen to what Esther said as she came out of her closet:

> *Go, gather all the Jews who are present in*
> *Shushan, and fast for me...and if I perish, I*
> *perish!* (Esther 4:16)

After three days, Esther dressed up and entered the inner court. There was something special about Esther, because, when Ahasuerus saw her, he held out his golden scepter, indicating that she was to come forward. (See Esther 5:1–2.)

You know, there comes a time when God calls each of us to a place of commitment, and we must say, "Even if everyone dislikes me or rejects me, I love You, Father, and I am going to obey You." Esther came out of the closet and made that commitment.

Did you notice that Esther did not just barge into the king's presence? Rather, she first prepared herself inwardly. I think that this is important to practice in our lives today. Whatever we do for God—whether witnessing, laying hands on people, giving out food, or simply interacting with other people, including our family members—we need to be spiritually in line with God's Word. Along with inward preparation, we also need to be prepared outwardly because the way we present ourselves has a great deal to do with how people respond to us.

Esther invited King Ahasuerus and Haman to have dinner with her. I am sure she was a very gracious hostess because the two men accepted a second invitation to join Esther for dinner the next night, also.

Haman, being a prideful man, was absolutely beside himself with excitement. He went home and told his wife,

> *Besides, Queen Esther invited no one but me to come in with the king to the banquet that she prepared; and tomorrow I am again invited by her, along with the king. Yet all this avails me nothing, so long as I see Mordecai the Jew sitting at the king's gate.* (Esther 5:12–13)

Haman's wife, Zezesh, perhaps not as impressed by his invitation, was only too pleased to advise her husband. *"Let a gallows be made, fifty cubits high, and in the morning suggest to the king that Mordecai be hanged on it; then go merrily with the king to the banquet"* (verse 14). Puffed up with pride, Haman followed his wife's evil counsel.

That very same night, King Ahasuerus couldn't sleep. *"So one was commanded to bring the book of the records of the chronicles; and they were read before the king"* (Esther 6:1). As the book of chronicles was read, the king was reminded of the attempt to assassinate him, and he was shown that it was Mordecai who had saved the day.

> *Then the king said, "What honor or dignity has been bestowed on Mordecai for this?" And the king's servants who attended him said, "Nothing has been done for him."* (verse 3)

Just then, Haman came in to talk with Ahasuerus about hanging Mordecai.

> *And the king asked him, "What shall be done for*
> *the man whom the king delights to honor?"*
> (Esther 6:6)

Haman had such a tremendous ego that he thought the king was referring to him.

> *For the man whom the king delights to honor,*
> *"let a royal robe be brought which the king has*
> *worn, and a horse on which the king has ridden,*
> *which has a royal crest placed on its head. Then*
> *let this robe and horse be delivered to the hand of*
> *one of the king's most noble princes, that he may*
> *array the man whom the king delights to honor.*
> *Then parade him on horseback through the city*
> *square, and proclaim before him: 'Thus shall it*
> *be done to the man whom the king delights to*
> *honor!'"* (verses 7–9)

Haman was delighted when the king agreed to his suggestion. Immediately, his delight turned to shock when the king said,

> *Hurry, take the robe and the horse, as you have*
> *suggested, and do so for Mordecai the Jew who*
> *sits within the king's gate! Leave nothing undone*
> *of all that you have spoken.* (verse 10)

I am sure that Mordecai was equally shocked when he saw Haman coming with all of that finery. He probably couldn't believe his ears when Haman led him through the city saying,

> *Thus shall it be done to the man whom the king delights to honor!* (Esther 6:11)

God has a way of turning situations around, doesn't He? If we Christians will come out of our closets of complacency and fulfill God's plans for our lives, great blessings will flow into our lives—and out through our lives to others.

Unfortunately for Haman, blessings didn't flow into his life. The king's servants took him to Esther's dinner party, and the king probably was on pins and needles wondering what Esther wanted. Finally, she said,

> *If I have found favor in your sight, O king, and if it pleases the king, let my life be given me at my petition, and my people at my request. For we have been sold, my people and I, to be destroyed, to be killed, and to be annihilated. Had we been sold as male and female slaves, I would have held my tongue, although the enemy could never compensate for the king's loss.* (verses 7:3–4)

Esther threw back the covers on her life and admitted her true identity. I love Esther's courage. Once she made up her mind, she didn't back down from her commitment.

When Haman heard what the queen had said, he knew he was doomed! King Ahasuerus was so upset that he went for a walk in the garden. Overwrought with worry, Haman ran to the queen and fell on the couch where she was reclining. I don't think Haman was trying to rape Esther, but when King Ahasuerus saw them, he sure thought so. *"Then the king said, "Will he also assault the queen while I am in the house?"* (Esther 7:8).

King Ahasuerus had Haman arrested, and he was hanged on the same gallows that he had arranged to be constructed for Mordecai. Then, the king gave all Haman's property to Esther. When Esther explained that Mordecai was her cousin, Ahasuerus honored him again, and Esther gave Haman's house to Mordecai.

Persian law did not allow a decree to be reversed, so the king wrote another letter granting the Jewish people the right to defend themselves against anyone who would try to kill them. Ahasuerus dispatched this second decree to every province, and *"the Jews had light and gladness, joy and honor"* (Esther 8:16).

On the date that had been designated as when the killing of the Jews would begin,

> *The Jews gathered together in their cities....And no one could withstand them, because fear of them fell upon all people.* (Esther 9:2)

All the Jewish people were saved because two people, Esther and Mordecai, came out of their closets and took their places as God's people.

COME OUT OF THE CLOSET

Likewise, the more you develop your relationship with God, the more your enemies will be at peace with you. Proverbs 16:7 says:

> *When a man's ways please the LORD, He makes even his enemies to be at peace with him.*

The more you develop your relationship with God, the more your enemies will be at peace with you.

When you come out of your closet of complacency and begin to show the love and power of God in your life, some of your enemies are going to become Christians— those who once were against you are going to be for you! Why? Because you are a Satan-proofer who is not afraid to let the light of Jesus Christ shine forth brightly in your life. And as people behold God's love through you, they will be drawn to Jesus, whose life, death, and resurrection make it possible for all men to receive everlasting life.

Chapter Five

Mark Your Household

Have you ever known someone who thought he was "hell-bound?" There are people who actually think that hell is their destiny. But I want to tell you that hell—the place of eternal torment—is not the destiny of people. Hell was prepared specifically for the devil and his angels. (See Matthew 25:41.)

Let me clarify the difference between *destiny* and *destine*. *Destiny* means "something to which a person or thing is destined: fortune; a predetermined course of events often held to be an irresistible power or agency." To *destine* means "to decree beforehand: predetermine; to designate, assign, or dedicate in advance; to direct, devise, or set apart for a specific purpose or place."

The primary point I want you to focus on here is that a *destiny* is usually inevitable or irresistible, while to *destine* is to set apart, to single out, to mark.

I received a powerful testimony from a man who calls himself the "Lone Ranger." He wrote: "I drove an 18-wheeler cross-country and did everything under the sun that was sinful, including drugs and alcohol, and I hired prostitutes regularly, even though I had a wife and three children at home."

Eventually, this man's wife died, and his children hated him and blamed him for their mother's death. The Lone Ranger stole the truck he'd been driving, and this fifty-year-old trucker ended up in prison.

By his lifestyle, this man certainly may have appeared to have been "hell-bound," but I want to tell you that God had *marked* the Lone Ranger. This man was *destined* to be born again! His new birth took place while he was in prison. God delivered him from his addictions and gave him a new wife and family. Now, he is the "New Lone Ranger," and he is a tremendous witness of God's mercy and grace.

MARK YOUR LOVED ONES

Jesus Christ has made it possible for people to reach the goal that God has destined us to achieve: eternal life. *"For God so loved the world that He gave His only begotten Son, that whoever believes in Him should not perish but have everlasting life"* (John 3:16).

All people are destined—set apart for a particular use—to subdue the earth and to be blessed. (See Genesis 1:27–28.) God created people in His own image, and we are destined—marked—to bear fruit and to govern the earth. But first, we must renew our minds and be conformed to the image of Christ. (See Romans 8:29; 12:2.) The renewing of our minds begins with repentance.

God desires all people to repent and become born again so that they can spend eternity with Him in heaven. This truth is conveyed in 2 Peter 3:9:

The Lord is not slack concerning His promise, as some count slackness, but is longsuffering toward us, not willing that any should perish but that all should come to repentance.

One definition of the word *repent* is "to change one's mind." God wants people to change their minds and become born again so that they will attain the goal that God has destined for all people—to live eternally with Jesus Christ. Isn't that why Jesus lived, died, and was resurrected? Yes, it is, and God decided before the foundation of the world that His precious human creations would be destined to receive eternal life through Christ Jesus.

> *God wants people to change their minds and become born again so that they will attain the goal that God has destined for all people—to live eternally with Jesus Christ.*

As Satan-proofers, we are charged with the job of marking our households for God. We are to single out or leave an impression upon our loved ones by setting ourselves in agreement with God's will for their lives.

Let me give you an example. For years, my husband, Wally, and I prayed for one of our relatives who was a homosexual. You know, many of our loved ones are caught up in bondage. If someone you love is involved in this terrible perversion, be sure to set yourself in agreement with God's view of the individual *sinner* rather than how you see the *sin.*

Please don't think that I am making light of homosexuality. It's a terrible sin; and the Bible says that *"the wages of sin is death"* (Romans 6:23). But God loves all people, including homosexuals—not their sin, but the actual people. While homosexuality is a sin, it is not an *unforgivable* sin. (See Luke 12:10.) So, let's begin praying for our loved ones so that they can get on the right track and receive what God has destined for their lives.

Wally and I *marked* this relative for Jesus. We set ourselves in agreement with God's will for his life. In Jesus' name, we persisted in rebuking Satan and binding the evil spirits that were involved. We regularly prayed for him and kept calling God's attention to his life. We also made an impression in his life by sharing God's Word with him and by allowing God's wonderful love to shine through us into his life. We never turned our backs on him, and God brought him through. One day, this man accepted Christ and was filled with the Spirit. Now he visits different churches and gives a tremendous testimony about God's power to deliver people from sin.

When you receive Christ as your Savior and become born again, you actually *mark* your loved ones to receive Christ as Savior, too: *"Believe on the Lord Jesus Christ, and you will be saved, you and your household"* (Acts 16:31).

When we Christians begin to Satan-proof our relatives, we actually take part in *marking* them, singling them out, or calling God's attention to them. It's easy to do. You can begin now to mark your household by praying, "Father, I thank You for all my loved ones, and I am marking them for You. In the mighty name of Jesus, I claim them to be born again, Spirit filled, and available for You to use in Your kingdom!"

There is something else God has destined for people that I want you to see: the infilling of His Holy Spirit.

That I will pour out of My Spirit on all flesh; your sons and your daughters shall prophesy, your young men shall see visions, your old men shall dream dreams. And on My menservants and on My maidservants I will pour out My Spirit in those days; and they shall prophesy.

(Acts 2:17–18)

What a tremendous time in the history of God's dealings with mankind! God will continue to pour out His Spirit until it has fallen upon "*all flesh.*" This means that the gift of God's glorious Spirit is available for *all* our loved ones.

When my daughter, Sarah, was just a baby, I marked her with Joel 2:28: "*And it shall come to pass afterward that I will pour out My Spirit on all flesh; your sons and your daughters shall prophesy, your old men shall dream dreams, your young men shall see visions.*"

I claimed this Scripture so that she would be born again and baptized in the Holy Spirit. One day, when she was four years old, Sarah said, "Mother, after you put me to bed tonight, I will wake up, and God is going to baptize me with the Holy Spirit, and I am going to pray in tongues." I thought, *Well, she's heard this in Sunday school, and she's saying it because she knows that it will please me.* But I didn't say that to her. Instead, I said, "Sarah, that will be wonderful!"

When I put her to bed, Sarah fell asleep immediately. Later, when I looked in on her, she was sitting up in her bed, smiling and *praying in tongues*! I had *marked* her to receive what God had destined for her—the gift of the Holy Spirit.

MARK YOUR CHILDREN FOR GOD

Marking our children for God is nothing new. Hannah marked her child for God, even before she became pregnant. *"Then she made a vow and said, 'O Lord of hosts, if You will...give Your maidservant a male child, then I will give him to the Lord all the days of his life'"* (1 Samuel 1:11).

I really admire Hannah's faith. She easily could have become discouraged and depressed, since her husband, Elkanah, had another wife, Peninnah, who already had children. Hannah had been unable to conceive, and, based on their custom then, she bore the shame of her barrenness with a heavy heart, but she prayed and wept bitterly to the Lord, who heard her prayers and answered them.

Perhaps you or someone you know desires to conceive a child, but the doctors have said that it is impossible. Be encouraged—when Wally and I got married, we wanted to have children, but we were told that we couldn't have a baby. Every doctor I visited told me that I had inherited sterility problems, and that it was therefore impossible for me to have a baby.

I have to admit, my faith wavered, but not Wally's. One day, I asked him, "How does your faith remain so firm?" He answered, "Because I have the faith of Jesus, Marilyn."

Thirteen years after we were married, I gave birth to a lovely baby girl.

Sarah certainly was our miracle baby, and we marked her life according to God's goals for His children. She has grown into a lovely, young woman—born again and Spirit-filled. She graduated from Oral Roberts University, and today she is a partner in my ministry, teaching on television as well as at churches and conferences around the world. (If I sound like a proud momma, it's because I am.)

Hannah also had gone to the Lord and said, "Lord, if You will give me a son, I will give him back to You, and he will serve You all the days of his life." God remembered Hannah. She and her husband had a son

111

and named him Samuel, which means "Heard of God." Samuel's mother really had marked his life with a godly goal to be a servant unto the Lord.

> **Did you know that when we dedicate our children to God, we are actually marking them for God's service?**

Did you know that when we dedicate our children to God, we are actually marking them for God's service? And, by faith, we also can mark our children before they are conceived. We can pray, "Father, I thank You for the children I will bring into this world. I am asking You to bless them, and I am claiming them for Your kingdom. They are not going to waiver to the right or to the left, but they will serve You forever."

What are we doing? We are saying, "God, I set myself in agreement with the eternal goals that You have set for my children's lives. I am going to pray, witness, and instruct them according to Your Word and trust You for the rest."

Proverbs 22:6 says, *"Train up a child in the way he should go, and when he is old he will not depart from it."* That's what Hannah did—she raised Samuel according to the Word of God and, at the appointed time, took Samuel to study under the high priest, Eli. It couldn't have been easy for Samuel living with Eli, because Eli definitely was not a very godly man. He certainly hadn't marked his children for the Lord, because they were the absolute pits! Nevertheless, it was necessary for Samuel to live in that environment.

Doesn't this bring to mind the terrible temptations that our children face today at school? On the television programs they want to watch? In the music they prefer? That's why we, as Christian parents, must Satan-proof our children by marking them for God at an early age. I believe that part of the reason Samuel did not backslide despite all the sin around him was that his mother had *marked* him for God. Hannah literally Satan-proofed Samuel, and we can do the same for our children today.

Mark Your Children with Prayer

One summer, a friend wrote to me and shared that she had lost her husband to a woman who was involved in witchcraft. The husband also had moved their sons in with this woman for four months. Satan really wanted to get a big victory out of the husband's sin, but...

God protected them [her sons] through my prayers and through the prayers of many other people. And praise God, they are now back with me and have accepted Jesus into their hearts. They are doing beautifully now.

This mother marked her children; she refused to allow the devil to steal them. How? With fervent prayer. James 5:16 says, *"The effective, fervent prayer of a righteous man avails much."* The word *fervent* can mean "very hot: glowing"—that's white-hot! With her white-hot prayers, this tenacious woman had welded her will to what God had destined for her sons, and the devil had to take his hands off!

If I were to ask you who prayed for your salvation, many of you probably would answer, "My mother" or "My grandmother." This person marked you for what God had destined for you to receive—salvation and the baptism of the Holy Spirit.

I love what Kenneth Copeland shared one time when he was visiting our church. He told us that, at one time, he had been uptight with God and had said, "God, You deal with me about every *little* thing I do. Other ministries get away with things, but You are always on my back." The Lord had spoken back to him, "The reason I am always on your back is because *your mother* is on My back!" Kenneth Copeland's mother had been praying white-hot prayers on her son's behalf, keeping him in the place where he could do what God had destined him to do.

Have you ever heard Kenneth Copeland's testimony? As a young man, he was as wild and rebellious as anyone I've ever heard of. He even rode a motorcycle down the halls of his high school because he'd seen his movie "idol" do it. Ken soon became involved in drugs, drinking, smoking, and the whole mess! But can you guess what his mother was doing whenever he came home at two or three o'clock in the morning? You guessed it—she was on her knees, marking her son for God's service. She said, "God, my son is marked. It doesn't matter what is going on around him; I have marked Ken for You, and he is not going to get away!"

Her white-hot prayers kept God's attention focused on her son. God turned Kenneth Copeland's life around, and he has become a powerful man of God.

Similarly, Hannah's white-hot prayers moved God to remember her, and she became pregnant with Samuel. (See 1 Samuel 1:19–20.) I believe Hannah continued to pray white-hot prayers for Samuel while he was with Eli. Undoubtedly, Samuel knew he was marked. He began to know the voice of God at a very young age, when *"the Lord called Samuel. And he answered, 'Here I am!'"* (1 Samuel 3:4).

Just as marking Samuel worked for Hannah and marking Kenneth Copeland worked for his mother, marking our children worked for Wally and me. And marking your children will work for you!

The prophet Jeremiah also had been marked, and he recorded the Lord's revelation to him about that truth: *"Before I formed you in the womb I knew you; before you were born I sanctified you; I ordained you a prophet to the nations"* (Jeremiah 1:5).

The word *sanctify* means "to set apart to a sacred purpose or to religious use." Doesn't that sound familiar? Remember, *destine* also means "to set apart." God

115

had destined Jeremiah to serve Him in the office of a prophet.

You know, I get so angry when I think about abortion. It truly is the most heinous crime committed against children. My heart weeps for the millions of babies killed, as well as for their mothers, who often suffer terrible emotional trauma afterward.

The Bible clearly shows that God has destined us before the foundation of the world to be made into His image, yet misguided people are deceiving themselves into believing that abortion is an acceptable form of birth control. I firmly believe that this horrendous practice has brought a curse upon our country.

Certainly, God loves women. And, of course, women have rights! But God also loves babies. We have absolutely no right to determine which babies should live or die, because *all* people are *marked* by God to receive eternal life through repentance and the new birth, as well as to receive the baptism of the Holy Spirit.

Folks, there is absolutely no question that abortion is murder. We Christians need to begin protecting our own sons and daughters against the possibility of being tricked by this devious lie of the devil. We need to begin Satan-proofing our children, grandchildren, and great-grandchildren until Jesus comes. We need to mark them for God and pray white-hot prayers on their behalf!

What if Jeremiah's mother had aborted him? We would have missed one of the greatest prophets of all time. And consider the words of the apostle Paul:

But when it pleased God, who separated me from my mother's womb and called me through His grace, to reveal His Son in me, that I might preach Him among the Gentiles.

(Galatians 1:15–16)

When had Paul been marked? While he was still in his mother's womb, just as Jeremiah had been centuries before. Now, I want to show you that even though we sometimes stray away from what God has destined for us, He will continue to deal with us until we come in line with His will for our lives.

> *Even though we sometimes stray away from what God has destined for us, He will continue to deal with us until we come in line with His will for our lives.*

Paul had an attitude that was totally ungodly. Paul was a legalist, a Pharisee. Even though he had been marked to preach the gospel of Jesus Christ, he did everything he could to destroy Christians.

When Paul was on his way to Damascus to persecute more Christians, he had a tremendous encounter with Christ Jesus. God knocked Paul to the ground and really got his attention. Then, He let Paul know that he had been marked, saying, in effect, "Paul, you are My marked man; now get up, go forward, and serve Me." (See Acts 9:3–6, 15.)

Paul did just that and went on to become the greatest apostle the world has ever known, aside from Jesus

Christ. Because of Paul's obedience to God, the door to salvation was opened to the Gentile (non-Jewish) world—and that includes you and me! Paul wrote at least fourteen books in the New Testament. God had destined Paul to be in His service, and God certainly did not allow Paul to escape from his calling.

There is a woman on my staff who, at a very young age, got into a sinful lifestyle of drug abuse and immorality. Her sister got saved and prayed for this woman, who eventually became born again and Spirit filled. God delivered her from her drug addiction and led her to Denver, where she continued to develop into a mature Christian and became a wonderful wife and mother! She has worked hard and has moved into an administrative position in my ministry. How did this happen? I believe that this staff member's sister Satan-proofed and marked her; by praying white-hot prayers, she welded herself to God's will for her sister's life.

Mark Your Children with Faith

I want to tell you about a man who was born during a time when Egypt's pharaoh had commanded that all male babies be thrown into the Nile River. Did you guess that I was referring to Moses? Moses' parents, Amram and Jochebed, refused to let their precious son be eaten by crocodiles.

By faith Moses, when he was born, was hidden three months by his parents, because they saw he

118

*was a beautiful child; and they were not afraid
of the king's command.* (Hebrews 11:23)

Moses' parents hid him in a basket, placing him
amidst the bullrushes where Pharaoh's daughter was
known to bathe. I love how Pharaoh's daughter reacted
when she unwrapped Moses: *"She saw the child, and
behold, the baby wept. So she had compassion on him,
and said, 'This is one of the Hebrews' children.'"* (Exodus
2:6). How did she know that Moses was a Hebrew? His
parents had *marked* Moses with circumcision, which
was God's mark for His covenant people.

I believe that when the devil looks at the child of a
Christian parent, it should cause him to say, "Oh, no!
This is a Christian's child who has been marked for
God's service. I am not going to waste my time here
because I know that this child has been Satan-proofed
by the white-hot prayers of his parents!"

When we study Hebrews 11, we see that it talks
about Moses' faith. Why did Moses have so much faith?
Because his parents had set the
mark of faith upon him.

If you want to Satan-proof
your children, then mark their
lives with faith. Let them see
you living by faith, reading God's
Word, praying, and attending
church. When you emphasize the
importance of serving God, your

**When you
emphasize the
importance of
serving God,
your children
will think it's
important, too.**

119

children will think it's important, too. They may not want to serve God right off the bat, but if you just hang in there, God will bring them through.

I want to encourage you to stop murmuring about your church in front of your children. Some of you go to church and then, on the way home, say, "Well, the greeters weren't too friendly," or "I really didn't like the message today," "The pastor is too loud when he worships," or some other gripe. Then, you wonder why your children do not want to go to church! It's because you've marked them with negative words. If you want to Satan-proof your children and mark them for God's service, then you'd better begin to speak well of your church so that your children will esteem it, too.

IT'S NEVER TOO LATE

I know that many of you are saying, "Well, Marilyn, I accepted Jesus as my Savior at a late age in life. My children have grown up; it's too late." Let me assure you, *it's never too late*. My mother became a Christian when I was nineteen, and that's when she began marking my brother and me. The first thing she did was to put Bibles on all the end tables and coffee tables in our house. Then, she posted Scriptures on the refrigerator door and around the sink—you should have seen our bathroom! All around the house, we read Scriptures such as, *"Do not marvel that I said to you, 'You must be born again'"* (John 3:7). What was my mother doing? She was marking us for God.

It doesn't matter whether you are a twenty-five-year-old parent or a ninety-five-year-old parent—begin to Satan-proof your children, regardless of their ages, by marking them with God's Word. (And don't forget those white-hot prayers!) Your children may think you are a little crazy, but that's all right—mark them, anyway!

Psalms 127:3–5 says:

Behold, children are a heritage from the LORD, the fruit of the womb is a reward. Like arrows in the hand of a warrior, so are the children of one's youth. Happy is the man who has his quiver full of them; they shall not be ashamed, but shall speak with their enemies in the gate.

Your children are your arrows, and they will go in the direction in which you point them. That is why the book of Proverbs instructs Christian parents to train their children in the way they should go. (See Proverbs 22:6.) When our children grow up, they won't depart from that training. Oh, they may stray for a while, but, eventually, they will return to the godly ways that we taught to them.

When you train your children according to God's Word, you are marking their direction. You're making them into straight arrows who will *"speak with their enemies in the gate.*" What does that mean? It means that when we mark our children, we are actually training them to stand against the devil. Eventually, our children will have to be able to deal with Satan. Ask yourself, *Am I preparing my children to stand against the fiery darts of the enemy?*

Do you remember what God said about Abraham before Isaac was born?

> *For I have known him, in order that he may command his children and his household after him, that they keep the way of the LORD, to do righteousness and justice, that the LORD may bring to Abraham what He has spoken to him.*
>
> (Genesis 18:19)

Abraham knew how important it was to teach his children about God. He knew that they needed to be marked, and his son, Isaac, certainly knew and served God.

It's so important that you teach your children to serve God. I want to show you three ways that you can mark your children: (1) through instruction, (2) by not provoking them to wrath, and (3) by treating them like your heavenly Father treats you.

Instructing Them

One way to mark your children is by teaching them. You say, "I bring them to Sunday school and to the midweek youth service." But, really, is two and a half hours a week enough instruction to prepare a child to stand against the wiles of the devil? I don't believe so. Our children must be taught the Word of God on a daily basis, and they also must be prayed with regularly. Daily family devotions at breakfast or dinner are an excellent way to do this.

Not Provoking Them

When we're marking our children, we must keep in mind what Paul wrote in Ephesians 6:4: *"And you, fathers, do not provoke your children to wrath, but bring them up in the training and admonition of the Lord."*

Of course, we are to discipline our children, but while we are correcting and shaping their wills, we must be careful not to break their spirits. The most important thing you can give your children is a good self-image. When your children need reproof, give it, but say, "I know you have misbehaved, and I am going to correct you by punishing you. But I love you, and I have confidence that you will not do this again." Always build them up.

You can keep Satan from taking over your child's emotions during times of correction by speaking wholesome words. Proverbs 15:1, 4 says, *"A soft answer turns away wrath, but a harsh word stirs up anger....A wholesome tongue is a tree of life, but perverseness in it breaks the spirit."* Criticism should always be constructive.

123

Remember, the ratio of encouragement to constructive criticism should be 90 percent encouragement to 10 percent criticism.

Treating Them as God Treats You

Another thing I want to share about marking your children is that you really need to treat them as God treats you. You say, "Marilyn, I don't know if I can handle that." I know that you can't in the natural; however; you have a new nature—you are being conformed to the image of Christ, so that makes you supernatural.

Let's see how God treats people: He is quick to forgive us, He loves us unconditionally, He never forsakes us, He is merciful and compassionate toward us, and He instructs us. In Christ, you can treat your children with the same love and concern that God has for you.

The last thing I want to say about marking your household has to do with believers living with unsaved spouses. Some of you get so "out of it" when it comes to your unsaved husband or wife. It's almost as if you suspect that your spouse may be the devil himself!

Remember the verse in 1 Corinthians we read earlier.

For the unbelieving husband is sanctified by the wife, and the unbelieving wife is sanctified by the husband; otherwise your children would be unclean, but now they are holy.

(1 Corinthians 7:14)

124

One believing spouse sanctifies—sets apart, marks, or calls God's attention to—the entire household. So, don't get all worked up if your spouse is unsaved. Just keep on Satan-proofing your loved ones and marking your household for God. Keep praying in the Holy Spirit, sending God those white-hot prayers. Keep allowing the love of Jesus to be shed abroad in your home. Keep speaking God's promises on your loved one's behalf. And, above all, stay in faith that God will move on His promises and do His perfect work in your loved one's life.

Chapter Six

Sowing and Reaping Miracles

W hat is a miracle? The dictionary defines *miracle* as "an extraordinary event manifesting divine intervention in human affairs." Miracles usually cause quite a stir in the lives of unbelievers, who have a difficult time accepting that there is an almighty God who sometimes upsets the natural order of things and performs miracles.

But we in the body of Christ know that when our heavenly Father performs a miracle—something beyond human or natural powers—He is simply making His presence known in the world. Therefore, we should accept miracles as a normal part of existence. In this chapter, I'm going to show you how you can experience God's miracle-working power when you begin to sow miracles into the lives of others.

Sometimes, I wonder why so few Christians experience the marvelous, miracle-working power of God in their lives. Walking in the miraculous should be a normal, everyday activity for Christians. Contrary to what many of you may think, miracles are not limited to the lives of people you believe to be "super Christians." Miracles occur in the lives of *ordinary* believers like you and me, who have been empowered by an *extraordinary* God to accomplish supernatural things.

When you received Christ as your Savior, you literally became a miracle. By the power of God, you entered into a new realm—a supernatural realm where the impossible becomes possible because of *faith*. What faith? Your faith in Jesus Christ, which allows you to stand on and live according to every word that comes forth from the mouth of God.

God's Word says believers will receive power: "*But you shall receive power when the Holy Spirit has come upon you*" (Acts 1:8). The Greek word here for "*power*" is *dunamis*, which means "miraculous power: ability, abundance, meaning, might; power, strength, violence, and mighty work" (*Strong's* #1411). We get the word *dynamite* from *dunamis*. God's *dunamis*—His miracle-working power—operating in your life will give you the ability to rise up and be strong in the Holy Spirit. You will become an explosive force in the spiritual realm.

If you are a Spirit-filled believer, then God's miracle-working power is within you. As a Satan-proofer, you are the recipient of an extraordinariness that surpasses all known human or natural powers: the Holy Spirit.

> **As a Satan-proofer, you are the recipient of an extraordinariness that surpasses all known human or natural powers: the Holy Spirit.**

There is another word for "power" that I want to look at. Let's consider Luke 10:19:

Behold, I give you the authority to trample on serpents and scorpions, and over all the power of the enemy, and nothing shall by any means hurt you.

In this Scripture, *"the power of the enemy"* is considered a miracle-working power.

The Bible gives many examples of demonic miracles being performed, beginning when the serpent spoke with Eve:

And [the serpent] *said to the woman, "Has God indeed said, 'You shall not eat of every tree of the garden'?"* (Genesis 3:1)

Can you imagine yourself having a conversation with a snake? That certainly would qualify as an extraordinary event that surpassed all known human powers—a miracle.

What about when Moses went before Pharaoh? The Egyptian sorcerers performed almost exactly the same miracles as did Moses—their rods became serpents, they caused the waters in the Nile River to turn to blood, and they caused frogs to come forth in a plague. (See Exodus 7:12, 22; 8:7.) These events, although extraordinary, definitely were not caused by God.

Now look back at Luke 10:19, where it says *"authority to trample on serpents and scorpions."* Here, the Greek word used for *"authority"* is *exousia*, which means "jurisdiction, liberty, power, right, strength" (*Strong's* #1849).

Satan's miracle-working *power* absolutely pales when compared to the *authority* of God. God has given authority *and* miracle-working power to believers to step all over the devil! And there is no question that when you begin to sow miracles into the lives of others, you are going to have to step on the devil's toes.

You received God's authority the moment you were born again, and, if you have been baptized in the Holy Spirit, you have been given God's miracle-working power. So, when you think about Satan-proofing your household by sowing miracles, I want you to know that God has equipped you to handle this challenge. Through Christ Jesus, you can do it!

OFF WITH THE OLD, ON WITH THE NEW

As I said earlier, Christians should be involved in the miraculous as a normal occurrence. What stops us? I believe God's power is hindered from operating in our lives when we become tangled up in our old nature. For various reasons, we sometimes harbor negative thoughts, attitudes, or emotions, such as unforgiveness, bitterness, anger, and resentment. These things are products of our old nature, and, believe me, they will stop God's miracle-working power from flowing freely in our lives.

Refuse to Be Ruled by Emotions

I want to talk to you about your emotions. Sometimes, it is easy to become negative. My heart almost breaks when I hear about the terrible suffering that some of you have experienced at the hands of others. You have reason to be angry and hurt—those are normal emotional responses.

But did you know that your emotions provide one of Satan's favorite playgrounds? You may have a normal emotional response to a situation, but Satan may invade your emotions, and then, before you know it, that normal response may turn into a sinful condition. We are commanded, however, not to sin in our anger: *"Be angry, and do not sin...nor give place to the devil"* (Ephesians 4:26–27).

If you want to sow miracles into the lives of others, then you will need to Satan-proof your emotions. God knows that you may become angry sometimes, but if you allow Satan to inflate your emotions, your anger may turn into hate. There may be times when you will experience disappointment. If you aren't careful, Satan can intensify your feelings, and you may become severely depressed and discouraged. But these negative things are part of our old nature, and we cannot experience God's miracle-working power if we allow them to master us. God wants us all to be Satan-proofers and to overcome our old nature so that we can operate in our new nature on a consistent basis. That's when believers

> **God wants us all to be Satan-proofers and to overcome our old nature so that we can operate in our new nature on a consistent basis.**

really begin to walk in the miraculous.

I want to tell you about a bona fide Satan-proofer who literally sowed miracles into her enemy's life. Years ago, a woman in our city came to me and shared how her daughter, a Bible school student in her thirties, had been stabbed to death. What a horrible tragedy! The mother told me how she had gone into deep depression as a result of her overwhelming grief. She'd soon become bitter toward God and built up a tremendous hatred for the murderer, who, after taking the lives of many more women, had finally been apprehended.

One Saturday night, God spoke to my friend and said, "If you don't forgive that murderer, I cannot forgive you, because if you don't forgive the trespasses of others, I can't forgive you of yours." Maybe she felt she had a right to be angry and hurt, but God insisted that she forgive the man.

So, this dear woman reached out to God and, by faith, forgave her daughter's murderer. The next day, God gave her an opportunity to act out her faith, and in doing so, she sowed a miracle into the man's life. The Gideons came to her church, and she made a contribution for Bibles. Then, she asked one of the Gideons to go and present a Bible personally to her daughter's murderer, who was in prison.

Yes, you guessed what happened next—God performed a miracle in the murderer's heart, and he became a victorious Christian. He literally became a missionary in that prison!

The woman sowed another miracle into this man's life by paying for his course materials when he enrolled in a correspondence Bible school. One day, she said to me, "Marilyn, the devil murdered my daughter, who was going to be a missionary, but God, in His great mercy, took my daughter's murderer and made him a missionary in a place where my daughter could never go!" Folks, *this was a miracle!*

How did it happen? This woman certainly had the right to be angry and hurt. That man had brutally murdered her daughter! Whether knowingly or unknowingly, he had allowed himself to be used by the devil and had harmed many people. But did my friend allow Satan to turn her anger into hate? No! She sowed a miracle into that man's life and reaped a tremendous miracle in her own life—the peace that passes all understanding, which brought her comfort about her daughter's death. That was extraordinary, and it certainly surpassed all human powers!

My friend took authority over any evil effort that the devil wanted to exert in her emotions. By faith, she stepped out of the realm of her emotions and into the realm of the supernatural—the miraculous! By doing so, she became a conduit for God's authority and miracle-working power to flow into the murderer's life. These miracles probably wouldn't have occurred if the woman had been operating according to her emotions. She sowed a miracle, and miracles continue to multiply each time another prisoner gets saved.

We all need to Satan-proof our emotions. Friends, let me say that one of the many roadblocks the devil will use to hinder you from receiving God's miracles is to keep you operating in your emotions—your old nature. However, through Christ Jesus, you have been given God's authority to step out of the realm of your emotions and into the realm of the supernatural—your new nature.

In your new nature, you will sow blessings and miracles into the lives of others—even your enemies. After all, your enemies (the human ones) are just victims who knowingly or unknowingly have allowed the devil to manipulate them into hurting you. When you begin to bless these people and sow miracles in their lives, then you will begin to walk in the miraculous on a more consistent basis in your own life.

You say, "Scripture says I have authority to tread on serpents and scorpions. I thought that meant the devil, not my emotions." You're right! But the devil can magnify your negative emotions to a dangerous level, and, if you aren't careful, your emotions can easily get out of control. When that happens, it's likely that you'll end up in a sinful condition.

My friend could have allowed the devil to invade her emotions and turn the normal grieving process into bitterness. There are few stings more deadly than that of a life lived in bitterness. And just as the poison from a snake (serpent) can destroy you, so, too, can bitterness and anger destroy your relationships, your hopes, and your dreams.

Let me encourage those of you who have had painful experiences with other people: you must begin to Satan-proof your emotions, keeping in mind that your heavenly Father is El Shaddai, "the Lord who is more than enough." His Holy Spirit *in you* makes you more than enough to overcome any negative feelings or thoughts that you may be harboring against someone. You will no longer focus on the terrible thing that may have been done to you. Instead, you'll focus on Jesus Christ, and you'll begin to operate in your new nature. Christ in you will take you out of the ordinary and into the extraordinary, and you'll respond to your adversaries with love. It's your *attitude* toward other people that determines your *altitude* in the miracle-working power of God.

> *His Holy Spirit in you makes you more than enough to overcome any negative feelings or thoughts that you may be harboring against someone.*

Sow the Miracle of Forgiveness

Probably all of us have had someone abuse us verbally, emotionally, or physically. And, if something bad happens to that person, our inclination is probably to think, *Goody, goody! That's what he deserves.* But that's really an ugly attitude that comes straight out of our old nature. The book of Proverbs cautions us against this attitude, saying, *"Do not rejoice when your enemy falls, and do not let your heart be glad when he stumbles; lest the Lord see it, and it displease Him"* (Proverbs 24:17–18).

This verse does not refer to our real enemy, the devil, but to other people who harm us. Regardless what the circumstances are, God says, "I know how you feel, but *don't rejoice* in another's catastrophes, for it will displease Me."

The Bible is quite clear when it talks about how we are to treat our enemies. Jesus said,

> *But I say to you, love your enemies, bless those who curse you, do good to those who hate you, and pray for those who spitefully use you and persecute you.* (Matthew 5:44)

We are to sow miracles into the lives of our enemies; we are to love them, bless them, pray for them, and do good to them. Now, your old nature doesn't want to do these things, but your new nature—the one you received when you were born again—wants to do good to all people.

136

God wants to set you free from the negative thinking and wrong attitudes that come out of your old nature. He wants you to become a Satan-proofer. He wants you to get out of the realm of your emotions so that you can reach into the supernatural and pull down miracles for yourself and for others, as well.

MIRACLES IN YOUR EMOTIONS

Many of you may be thinking right now, *I just can't control my emotions.* But that simply is not true, because, in Christ, you can do all things. (See Philippians 4:13.) The Bible contains many examples of believers who chose to serve God rather than their emotions—and they aren't all big names like Jesus, Elijah, Moses, or Paul, either. Some of their names are not even mentioned—Naaman's wife's handmaiden, for instance. At one time in Israel's history, Syria had repeatedly come down and attacked God's people. The commander-in-chief of the Syrian army was a man named Naaman. (See 2 Kings 5:1.) On one of his campaigns against Israel, the Syrians had taken captive a little Jewish girl, who became a servant to Naaman's wife.

Imagine the emotional trauma this young girl must have experienced being kidnapped from her home and forced into slavery by the Syrians. Then, one day, she learned that her mistress's husband had the dread disease leprosy. It must have been difficult for her to resist the urge to rejoice at Naaman's calamity and say, "He stole me from my parents, my church, and my life. He deserves to have leprosy because he killed a lot of my relatives!" But she didn't rejoice. Instead, she said to her mistress, *"If only my master were with the prophet who is in Samaria! For he would heal him of his leprosy"* (2 Kings 5:3).

I want to compare Naaman's wife's servant's response with the response of a woman who was forced to endure a different kind of slavery. One of my Bible school students shared that from the age of seven to the age of sixteen, she had been sexually abused by her stepmother's brother. Many times, she went to her parents and told them how she had been enslaved to this man's sickening behavior, but they didn't believe her. She became pregnant and, through some extremely painful circumstances, miscarried her baby.

I praise God that this young woman eventually got out of that abusive environment, and that, today, she is born again and Spirit filled. She has done missionary work in Africa, Japan, Korea, and the Virgin Islands. It took time, but God has healed her emotionally and physically from the damage inflicted upon her while she was growing up.

One day, the step-uncle who had abused her fell from a ladder and injured himself; his doctors said he would never walk again. Now, watch how God performed a miracle in this situation. If the young woman had allowed herself to operate out of her old nature, she could have really rejoiced at the calamity of the man who had destroyed her precious childhood. Instead, she sowed a miracle into his life—she forgave her abuser! Then, she led him to the Lord! Today, he, his wife, and most of their children have been saved and are serving God!

Quite honestly, most of us want to see God's miracles occurring in our own lives but rarely want to sow miracles into the lives of other people—especially the lives of our enemies. But, let me tell you, sowing and reaping and asking for miracles go together like Siamese twins.

Look at what happened when Naaman's wife's little Jewish servant resisted the urge to snicker and gloat over Naaman's mishap. She sowed a miracle into Naaman's life by suggesting that he go and see the prophet, Elisha. Naaman visited Elisha and was miraculously healed of leprosy. But he wasn't just healed of the disease. The greater miracle occurred in Naaman's heart, for *"he returned to the man of God, he and all his aides, and came and stood before him; and he said, 'Indeed, now I know that there is no God in all the earth, except in Israel'"* (2 Kings 5:15).

Naaman is never mentioned again as one who led an attack against Israel. Why? Because his life was changed, and he no longer was Israel's enemy. *"When a man's ways please the Lord, He makes even his enemies to be at peace with him"* (Proverbs 16:7).

You know, sometimes, we believers get into a peculiar mind-set. We see God's wonderful, miracle-working power in action in someone else's life but refuse to accept miracles in our own lives.

One man in our church found it difficult to believe that divine healing flowed so easily through our congregation. He didn't believe that people could be in severe pain one moment and be completely pain-free the next. Then, he injured his leg. When he came to church, his leg was swollen, blue, and throbbing with pain. The Holy Spirit led us into a healing service, and—you guessed it—our friend, who had been in severe pain one moment, was completely pain-free the next.

God's miracle-working power didn't affect the Syrian king. He continued to attack Israel again and again. However, his armies never succeeded in surprising the Israelites—they always seemed to know when and where their enemy was going to attack. It would have been natural for the Syrian king to assume there was a traitor in his camp. He demanded to know, "Who's the dirty traitor?" And a servant answered, *"None, my lord, O king; but Elisha, the prophet who is in Israel, tells the king of Israel the words that you speak in your bedroom"* (2 Kings 6:12).

Elisha certainly was a tremendous man of faith. By faith, Elisha heard the king making secret plans to attack Israel in the privacy of the royal bedroom! The Bible says, *"The secret things belong to the Lord our*

SOWING AND REAPING MIRACLES

God, but those things which are revealed belong to us" (Deuteronomy 29:29).

Because God knows the secret plots of men, He can lead us by His Spirit so that we won't fall into the enemy's snares. I think we Christians sometimes believe that if we don't bang our enemies around, our enemies will bang us around. But I am going to tell you that if you stay true to God, He will show you the secrets of your enemies and protect you

> **Because God knows the secret plots of men, He can lead us by His Spirit so that we won't fall into the enemy's snares.**

from them. And what does God want you to do with what He reveals to you about your enemies? He wants you to bless them, to pray for them, and to sow miracles into their lives. The ability to do these things comes out of our new nature, our faith nature.

I once received a letter from a woman in Dallas describing how God had dealt with her about being involved in an adult book store business. She terminated her involvement and then challenged her husband to do the same. Yet, he refused and chose to stay involved in pornography rather than maintaining his marriage to this courageous Christian lady. She said in her letter,

> While my husband and I were separated, he became acquainted with a girl who was a hooker and a cocaine addict. At first, I was angry,

bitter, and really hurt. My prayers seemed to go unanswered.

Then, one day a voice spoke to me, saying, "Read about forgiveness! I prayed a prayer and spoke my husband's name first, and then the girl's name, forgiving them both. The peace and love and joy I found and felt at that moment couldn't be described. It was truly the peace that passes all understanding. After that prayer, God began to open my eyes and heart for this girl. For thirteen months I prayed for her—eating, sleeping, and breathing for her salvation.

Eventually, the woman's marriage was restored, and the "other woman" ended up in prison. While she was imprisoned, this woman received Christ as her Savior and began witnessing to the prison guards and inmates!

Do you see what happened here? She was betrayed by her husband and injured by another woman. She allowed the devil to invade her normal emotional reaction and cause it to escalate into bitterness and resentment, which were part of her old nature. The minute that she got into her old nature, her prayers went unanswered. Folks, as long as you are in your old nature, you will not experience God's miracle-working power in your life.

When this woman stepped out of the realm of her emotions and into the realm of the supernatural, God intervened in her situation and brought about a change.

Was it an easy thing for her to accomplish? No, but in her new nature—the Christlike nature—loving her enemy became possible.

DIVINE PROTECTION

When you begin to sow miracles into the lives of your "enemies," don't be surprised when the devil really zeroes in on you. That Syrian king ordered his servants to find Elisha, saying, *"'Go and see where he is, that I may send and get him.' And it was told him, saying, 'Surely he is in Dothan'"* (2 Kings 6:13).

Elisha was in the city of Dothan, which means "a double decree." When you sow a miracle into the life of someone else, you'll get a double miracle—one in his life and one in your life, too.

I am always amazed that the Syrian king felt it necessary to send so many soldiers to capture Elisha: *"Therefore he sent horses and chariots and a great army there, and they came by night and surrounded the city"* (2 Kings 6:14).

All these soldiers were trying to sneak up on Elisha in the middle of the night, but, remember—God was revealing their plans to Elisha. Although he knew they were coming, do you think Elisha was nervous? No way! Elisha was operating in the supernatural realm, the faith realm. Now, his servant was the one who had the problem. He was absolutely terrified.

Look at how lovingly Elisha dealt with his servant. Elisha didn't jump down his throat saying, "You're not supposed to be afraid. Haven't you been listening to what I have been teaching you?" Rather, Elisha sowed a miracle into his servant's life.

> *And Elisha prayed, and said, "Lord, I pray, open his eyes that he may see." Then the Lord opened the eyes of the young man, and he saw. And behold, the mountain was full of horses and chariots of fire all around Elisha.* (2 Kings 6:17)

Elisha prayed for a miracle, and prayer is the major means by which you are going to see God's miracle-working power flow into your life, too. Elijah sowed a miracle through prayer, and this young servant saw the divine protection that God has for His people. When the servant looked up, he saw that the mountain was full of horses and chariots of fire! Surely, he recalled Elijah's having been taken up to heaven in a chariot of fire. (See 2 Kings 2:11.) Now he was seeing firsthand that God's chariots of fire were there for Elisha, too. Did you notice that Elisha didn't pray for himself to see God's divine protection? Elisha operated in a supernatural realm and, by faith, knew that God's miracle-working power would work in his circumstances, just as it had worked in Elijah's.

When we are facing new challenges, we need to keep in mind that the same God who delivered us in the past certainly is able to deliver us in the present. Even though we may not always be able to see the end results, we can be certain that God's protection is around His people. In the book of Romans, Paul raised this very profound point: *"If God is for us, who can be against us?"* (Romans 8:31).

> **When we are facing new challenges, we need to keep in mind that the same God who delivered us in the past certainly is able to deliver us in the present.**

The answer, of course, is no one! There will always be more going for God's people than going against them. Consider Elisha—the Syrians had surrounded the city to capture him. Can you imagine a whole army coming to get one little man? It sounds almost funny. The king of Syria was obviously afraid of Elisha.

Did you know that the devil is afraid of you? One little Christian frightens Satan silly. He knows that when you begin to operate in your new nature—your faith nature—and begin to walk in the authority and miracle-working power of God, then he's had it!

Elisha prayed for another miracle: *"'Strike this people, I pray, with blindness.' And* [God] *struck them with blindness according to the word of Elisha"* (2 Kings 6:18).

Isn't it interesting that God opened the eyes of Elisha's servant and then closed the eyes of Elisha's enemies? I can remember times when it seemed that God closed the eyes of government officials when my ministry team took the Word of God into communist countries. One time, we were taking Bibles into Poland. We also wanted to make a video there, so we had thirteen pieces of video equipment with us. We had been warned that the customs officers might confiscate our equipment when we got to Warsaw because the Polish government didn't like the idea of Christians coming into their country making videos. However, we believed that God was leading us. So, before we got off the plane, we prayed, "Lord, help us to come through and get all our videos in and out quickly and safely—even if you have to blind the eyes of the customs people."

The customs officer was a woman. She had an ugly attitude and really gave me a hard time. But when she saw my associate who had the thirteen pieces of video equipment, she smiled sweetly at him and told him to go through.

I don't believe she even saw the equipment. I believe God closed her eyes to the equipment that we needed to use to perform what He had called us to do in Poland.

Similarly, God had blinded the Syrian soldiers; then, Elisha tricked them into going to Samaria, the capital of Israel. When they arrived, Israel's king, Jehoram, said to Elisha, *"My father, shall I kill them? Shall I kill them?"* (2 Kings 6:21).

Jehoram probably thought, *What an opportunity to kill all these Syrians. They are like sitting ducks!* That would have been a natural response. But God's Word tells us to love our enemies. We are to pray for them, to bless them, and to do good to them. (See Luke 6:27–28.) And, don't forget, it was God's miracle-working power that had brought the enemy to the king's front door in the first place. Why had God done that? To show forth His marvelous mercy. You see, the Lord is not only a friend to believers; He is also a friend to sinners. God has destined *all* people to come to repentance so that they all can be born again and Spirit filled.

When Jehoram indicated his desire to kill the Syrians, Elisha answered him,

You shall not kill them. Would you kill those whom you have taken captive with your sword and your bow? Set food and water before them, that they may eat and drink and go to their master. Then he prepared a great feast for them; and after they ate and drank, he sent them away and they went to their master. So the bands of Syrian raiders came no more into the land of Israel.

(2 Kings 6:22–23)

Doesn't God's Word tell us that if our enemy is hungry, we are to feed him and to give him water, if he is thirsty? If you can pray for your enemies and sow

147

miracles into their lives, that is, in itself, a miracle. It means that you are a Satan-proofer doing extraordinary things that surpass human power. You're operating out of your new nature, and, through Jesus Christ, you're accomplishing the miraculous.

You know, if you are looking for a double feast of God's miracle-working power in your life, you must come out of your old nature. Elisha could have led those blind men right over the edge of a cliff or even said to Jehoram, "Yes! Go ahead and kill them." Either of those actions certainly would have been the natural thing to do.

However, Elisha was not operating in the natural. He was operating in the supernatural, and he showed forth God's marvelous mercies to Israel's enemies. They fed the Syrian army and sent them home. That must have been a huge grocery bill, but the choice to walk in the miraculous and to sow love, peace, joy, and righteousness into the lives of others always costs something. Salvation is free, but serving the Lord will cost you something. Do you know what it costs? It costs you your old nature, which really isn't a terribly big price to pay in order to see God's wonderful miracles occurring in your life.

Chapter Seven

Wisdom for Your Future

I really get inspired when I read the book of Hebrews. Chapter 11 is sometimes referred to as the "Hall of Fame" for our biblical heroes of the faith. It absolutely overflows with examples of ordinary people who walked in godly wisdom. They put their faith in an extraordinary God and supernaturally Satan-proofed their futures.

Through the lives of Abraham, Isaac, Jacob, and Joseph, we are going to see how we can walk in godly wisdom and, *by faith*, secure our futures. You may say, "Marilyn I want to secure my family's I future, but I don't know how to get godly wisdom."

> *If any of you lacks wisdom, let him ask of God, who gives to all liberally and without reproach, and it will be given to him.* (James 1:5)

The Greek word used here for *wisdom* means "a clarity in spiritual things." In order to secure your future, you need to get a better understanding of the things of God. You need to know how to secure your future according to God's plan for your life. And to know what God has planned for you and your loved ones, you'll have to seek Him.

We live in uncertain times for our personal lives and the world alike. Some people live in a constant state of fear because they focus on the statistics on crime, abortion, and substance abuse, which continue to increase at an alarming rate. Many of these people have experienced firsthand the heartbreaking results of the demise of the first institution God established—marriage. People look at all the unrest in the world and panic, wondering, *Oh, dear, what's going on? Things are getting worse and worse; what will become of us?*

Praise God! Why? Because, in the midst of all this chaos, you, the believer, don't have to worry! You are a covenant child of *El Elyon*, the Most High God; you can have the highest confidence because God has big plans for your future. However, you have to begin walking in faith and in God's wisdom if you want to see His plans manifested in your future.

> **When you live your life with an attitude of worship, you put yourself in a position to inherit everything that God has destined for you.**

There are three specific blessings that we should consider when we talk about securing our futures: material blessings, inheritance, and victory. Despite the circumstances around you, God wants you to know that you, His child, have been *blessed*. When you live your life with an attitude of worship, you put yourself in a position to inherit everything that God has destined for you—eternal life, baptism in the Holy Spirit, and being conformed into the wonderful image of Jesus Christ. In the image of Christ, you'll subdue the earth (your environment) and bear the fruit that accompanies victorious living, such as good health, financial security, peace of mind, and the joy of the Lord.

Some of you may think, *Well, I'm born again and I love the Lord, but my health is bad, my finances are a mess, and my nerves are just about shot!* Do you wonder why you don't seem to be able to get it together and walk in prosperity like other Christians? Be encouraged, because, although the above may describe where you are today, I believe that when you begin to walk in faith and godly wisdom, your life, health, and finances are going to do a complete turnaround. Your future will be secured according to God's desires for your life, and you can rest assured that He plans for you to be victorious over your circumstances.

WALK IN GODLY WISDOM

As you begin to focus more intently on God's will for you and your loved ones and begin to seek Him more seriously through prayer, Bible study, and the application of God's Word, then you'll start to become a

Satan-proofer. And there is absolutely no question that your life will change, and your future will be secured in God's Word.

Again, the key to a secured future is walking in godly wisdom. Let's get very practical. What should you do after you have prayed and asked God for wisdom? You spend a lot of time with God, and He shows you exactly how to apply the Scriptures to your circumstances. That's how you begin to secure your future by faith and godly wisdom.

The Bible gives us great examples of individuals who secured their futures by faith.

> *By faith Isaac blessed Jacob and Esau concerning things to come. By faith Jacob, when he was dying, blessed each of the sons of Joseph, and worshiped, leaning on the top of his staff. By faith Joseph, when he was dying, made mention of the departure of the children of Israel, and gave instructions concerning his bones.*
>
> (Hebrews 11:20–22)

All these men secured their futures *by faith*! Where did they put their faith? In God. And when they began to step out in His Word and His wisdom, they secured a future for themselves and for their loved ones.

I believe Abraham had a pretty clear understanding of spiritual things. When he walked in godly wisdom, he secured the future for himself, his descendants, and, potentially, the whole world. Abraham is sometimes called the "Father of Faith," and there is no question that he was a man of supernatural faith. Yet, even though he had faith, Abraham did not always walk in godly wisdom, and when he didn't, the results were disastrous. When he walked in faith, however, the results were wonderful.

Abraham (Abram at that time) acted in great faith when he first encountered God and received instructions to leave his home in Haran and travel to an unknown destination. Can you imagine the conversation that might have occurred between Abram and his wife (Sarai, not Sarah, at that time) that night?

"Sarai, God told me to leave Haran."

"All right, Abram, but where are we going?"

"Oh, I don't know; God didn't say. But He did say that through me, all the families of the earth would be blessed." (See Genesis 12:1–3.)

Obediently, Abram followed God's instructions.

So Abram departed as the LORD had spoken to him, and Lot went with him. And Abram was seventy-five years old when he departed from Haran. (Genesis 12:4)

When you think about this seventy-five-year-old man and his household, you might be picturing some little band of nomads trudging off through the countryside. But, actually, Abraham had a huge household.

153

He had many servants and workers, including at least 318 trained soldiers, along with their wives and families. (See Genesis 14:14.) And that isn't counting Lot's household! So, when Abraham packed up his household and left Haran, he may have been leading a caravan of several thousand people. Abraham was wise enough to recognize and to obey God.

Listen to the Lord's Instructions

I love to hear testimonies from my Bible school students and from the members of my staff. There are so many cases where God has literally called people to pack up and move to Denver. Before he joined our staff, one of our pastors called my husband and me to say that he and his wife believed God was calling them to Denver to become involved in our ministry. At that time, there were no positions available, but they were still convinced that Denver was in God's plan for their future.

So, we all prayed about it. Not long after their phone call, an opening became available that seemed tailor-made for their abilities. They moved their family to Denver, and the husband now heads up our pastoral care ministry. This couple continues to walk in God's wisdom for their future, and they have been a tremendous blessing to us.

Now, I want you to know that you will always have a choice as to whether you will walk wisely in spiritual things. This couple could have rationalized God's instructions to them about moving; after all, they pastored a thriving church in California. Similarly, Abraham could have said, "Oh, I'm just not sure; maybe that wasn't God's voice. I'd better stay here in Haran."

You will always have a choice as to whether you will walk wisely in spiritual things.

But Abraham didn't say that. He had tremendous faith in God, which really was a supernatural thing, considering that he had been an idol worshipper. He didn't have a Bible; there were no church services to attend; no evangelist came to Abraham's city to get him saved. No, it was God's spoken Word that convicted Abraham. Abraham stepped out on the Word by faith and thereby secured a future—not only for himself, but also for all the people who depended upon him. Abraham served God, and he demanded that his entire household serve God along with him. (See Genesis 18:19.)

As I said earlier, Abraham was a man of great faith, but he didn't always walk in godly wisdom. There is a difference between walking in faith and walking in wisdom. One time, after Abraham had been living in Canaan for about ten years, Sarah began to get nervous because she and Abraham hadn't conceived a child. She may have been thinking about God's promise that all the families on earth would be blessed through Abraham. How could that happen unless a child was born to Abraham?

Then, Sarah got an idea that she thought would "speed up" God's timetable. The ungodly customs of the day sanctioned a way of conceiving an heir to whom one would bequeath his property that sounds unusual today. Accordingly, Sarah cooked up a scheme whereby Abraham would become sexually involved with Hagar, her Egyptian servant; their union would produce an heir for Abraham.

When Abraham heard the idea, he could have said, "No, Sarah, God didn't tell me to do things that way. We are going to trust God's Word to instruct us in our plans for the future." However, we know that Abraham went along with Sarah's kooky idea, and he and Hagar produced a son named Ishmael. Abraham and Sarah probably thought that they had secured their future; however, they were operating in flesh, not faith, and Ishmael was not the promised seed—Isaac was.

In that situation, Abraham was not walking in God's wisdom. He may have had great faith to leave his homeland and to follow God into parts unknown, but faith without wisdom can cause big trouble for a believer.

The Bible indicates that about ten years passed before God communicated with Abraham again. (See Genesis 17:1.) This time, God appeared to Abraham and told him to walk before Him and be perfect. In other words, "Abraham, do things My way, and be sincere and upright in your walk."

It is imperative that we Christians do things God's way if we want to Satan-proof our lives and secure our futures. As long as Abraham did things his way, disaster followed, but when he began to walk in faith and godly wisdom for his circumstances, blessings followed.

Abraham and Sarah finally got on the tight track. Together, they had a son, Isaac. However, the tension between Sarah and Hagar continued to grow until Abraham was forced to expel Hagar and his firstborn son, Ishmael, from his household. Sometimes, I feel sorry for Hagar and Ishmael. But, then, I remember that God is wonderful and loves all people. When Hagar and Ishmael began to cry out to God, He showed forth His marvelous mercies and secured their futures with His provisions. (See Genesis 21:14–19.)

WISDOM FOR MATERIAL SECURITY

Abraham and Sarah raised Isaac according to God's Word, and just before Abraham died, he blessed Isaac with his substance: *"Abraham gave all that he had to Isaac"* (Genesis 25:5).

It's interesting to note that even though Abraham had other sons by his second wife, Keturah, Abraham gave the bulk of his wealth to Isaac, his son with Sarah. Abraham didn't ignore his other children—he gave them gifts, too—but he also sent them away from Isaac. Abraham's experience with Hagar and Ishmael probably had taught him a lesson about strife, and so he used godly wisdom in securing Isaac's future and keeping all his brothers from laying claim to Isaac's inheritance.

After Abraham died, God blessed Isaac and secured his future: *"And it came to pass, after the death of Abraham, that God blessed his son Isaac. And Isaac dwelt at Beer Lahai Roi"* (Genesis 25:11). The Hebrew definition of *Beer Lahai Roi* is "well of the Living One seeing me." Isaac was really blessed, but who had actually blessed his future? When Abraham had been alive, he'd done all he could for his son, but it was God who actually blessed Isaac's future. Abraham had sown the seeds; he'd prayed about Isaac and prepared his son to receive God's future plans. Although Abraham had claimed blessings for Isaac, it was God who really gave life to Isaac's future.

One morning, I was praying out on our back porch. I remember that it was so pretty that summer, and it just seemed as if the Lord had opened up the heavens to me while I was praying. He asked me, "Did you know that when you pray, you are laying up treasures in heaven?" I thought, *Well, Father, I know we say that about our giving, but I didn't know about prayers.* God went on to explain that when I prayed, it was as if I was depositing into a bank account. All the prayers I deposited would come down upon the people I had prayed for—blessings would come upon their lives as they drew out of my prayer account. I have seen some of my prayers come to pass, but, if Jesus tarries, some may not manifest until after I die.

The prayers we pray in the present will bless people in the future. When believers are walking in godly wisdom, they have strong, consistent prayer lives. Prayer will bring you into a more intimate relationship with your heavenly Father,

> *The prayers we pray in the present will bless people in the future.*

and, during those precious times of fellowship, God will share some wonderful revelations about how to apply His Word to your circumstances.

YOUR EXAMPLE CAN MAKE A DIFFERENCE

I want to look at Isaac's life to see if his future was secured by his father's blessings.

> *Isaac was forty years old when he took Rebekah as wife....Now Isaac pleaded with the LORD for his wife, because she was barren; and the LORD granted his plea, and Rebekah his wife conceived.* (Genesis 25:20, 21)

Doesn't this sound familiar? Isaac's mother had been barren, and, now, his wife, Rebekah, was barren. What did Isaac do? He prayed to God on Rebekah's behalf. No doubt, Abraham and Sarah had shared with Isaac their testimony again and again of how God had

159

blessed them with him, their miracle baby. They had secured Isaac's future by sharing their faith with him. When Isaac was confronted with a similar problem, he knew enough about spiritual things to pray and believe God for a baby.

Allowing our children to see us walking diligently in faith and conducting our lives according to godly wisdom is the best example we can model because it sets the tone for their spiritual growth. You can see the principle of sowing and reaping in action here. If you sow spiritual things like faith and godly wisdom into your children's futures, then they will reap futures rooted in faith and godly wisdom. However, if you sow worldly things like chance and luck into your children's futures, then they will be rooted in that same kind of instability.

We Christians must begin Satan-proofing our households and preparing our children to live diligently in the wisdom of God. Yet, we simply cannot pass along to our children what we ourselves do not have. So, if you need wisdom (and, quite frankly, we all do), ask God. Then, begin to seek Him more diligently through prayer and reading His Word. You will be pleasantly surprised at the difference godly wisdom makes in your life today and in your future.

One of my favorite Scriptures is Hebrews 11:6: *"But without faith it is impossible to please Him, for he who comes to God must believe that He is, and that*

He is a rewarder of those who diligently seek Him." I pray this Scripture regularly. There are certain things that I am believing God for, but, sometimes, the answer or reward seems to take forever to arrive. So, I continue reminding myself that God is a rewarder of those who diligently seek Him. When I set aside time to spend with God every day, I know that He is going to reward me for the time I spend with Him.

> **When I set aside time to spend with God every day, I know that He is going to reward me for the time I spend with Him.**

Maybe you need victory in your life, or your spouse or your children have a problem that they need to overcome. Let me encourage you to be diligent in seeking God—that's wisdom! When you continue to pray and trust God, He will reward you, and your family will be blessed to live victoriously. Remember, diligence brings reward, and a lack of diligence brings nothing.

If you want to Satan-proof your loved ones, then you will need to set aside a special time each day for prayer—genuine prayer that seeks God. Then, God will not only reward you with His presence but also bless you because you spent time seeking Him. Wow! That's a double-portion blessing! In addition, when your children see that spending time in God's presence is a primary part of your life, they, too, will begin to understand the importance of living in faith and walking in godly wisdom.

There is a woman I know who inspires me with her tremendous faith for the salvation of her loved ones. This woman is absolutely determined that her entire family will come into the kingdom of God. She spends a lot of time seeking God's wisdom, which she really needs, because it takes godly wisdom to live with an unsaved spouse.

This woman's bulldog faith secured her son's future when he was a senior in high school. All through his high school years, he had mostly fooled around. Although he was very bright and was capable of getting good grades, he never quite lived up to his potential. Then, during his final semester of school, he told his parents that he didn't really feel like going to school. He had given up hope of succeeding.

Despite her son's poor academic performance, my friend encouraged him to stay in school. She was absolutely convinced of his ability to graduate with his class, and she told him, "In Genesis, it says that all men are made in the image and likeness of God. Son, I don't care what anybody says about you; I choose right now to see the image of God in you. That's all I am going to look at."

This mother had faith in God for her son, and she walked in godly wisdom and applied the Word to the situation. The young man agreed to return to school, and God sent a Christian teacher to encourage him.

I believe that this mother's supernatural faith secured her son's academic future. Soon, he began to have confidence in himself. He began to work diligently, carrying a full load of courses plus one extra class, and he graduated with his head held high.

The woman Satan-proofed her son by securing his future, and the result was victory. In the future, if her son should ever become discouraged again, I believe he will remember his mother's example, and God will bring him through all his difficult times.

Let's look back at how Abraham's example of godly wisdom and faith took root in Isaac's life. When Isaac was old and nearing death, he followed his father's example and blessed his children. I believe there is wisdom in blessing our children with our substance, as well as our mouths. Many parents have the attitude that says, "I never had it easy; I've always worked and earned my way—let my children do the same."

I agree wholeheartedly that our children should be responsible for themselves, and that we need to prepare our children to live independently. It's wise for parents to have sufficient savings and life insurance so that their children will have the resources to pay for a college education and other important things, even if their parents are no longer alive. Educational security is an important part of the futures of your children and grandchildren.

Isaac saw the wisdom in his father's actions, and he wanted to do the same for his two sons, Jacob and Esau. Before he died, Isaac called Esau to him and said, "Esau, go cook me some savory meat, because I want to bless you before I die." (See Genesis 27:4.). Esau probably was very excited. He had already lost his birthright blessing through his own foolishness (see Genesis 25:29–34), and he had no intention of losing the firstborn blessing, as well. So, he ran out to kill the meat he needed to make a stew for his aging father.

> **You can operate in godly wisdom only when you are living according to God's Word.**

It sounds like everything was in order, except for one thing: Isaac was not walking in godly wisdom. You can operate in godly wisdom only when you are living according to God's Word.

The first born blessing was not part of God's plan for Esau, and He told Rebekah as much before her sons were even born:

And the LORD said to her: "Two nations are in your womb, two peoples shall be separated from your body; one people shall be stronger than the other, and the older shall serve the younger."

(Genesis 25:23)

From the start, God's plan was that the younger son would be blessed. The younger son was Jacob, not Esau; so, despite Isaac's seemingly good intentions, he was simply out of God's will when he attempted to bless Esau. The firstborn blessing had to do with rulership, prosperity, and priestly authority. Isaac was unwise in choosing to give that blessing to Esau when God's choice was Jacob. Isaac's ungodly actions nearly resulted in his younger son's death, because Esau certainly wanted to kill Jacob—especially since Jacob manipulated the circumstances, deceived Isaac, and received the first born blessing Isaac had intended for Esau.

Jacob had to flee for his life, and he went to live with his Uncle Laban. Poor Jacob had such a hard time. Laban changed Jacob's wages ten times and tricked him into marrying Leah, when the daughter Jacob really loved was Rachel. But I noticed that Jacob always came out smelling like a rose! Why? Because his father had secured his future by prophesying the blessings of God on Jacob's life.

Folks, we can have faith for our children's futures. When we parents begin to walk in faith and govern our actions by godly wisdom, then God's blessings will come upon our lives—and our children's lives, as well.

THE HARVEST

There is absolutely no question that you will reap what you sow. Maybe it will be a fast crop, and you'll reap it tomorrow or a month from now. Or, maybe your children will reap what you have sown long after your death. But you will always secure your future when you sow seeds of faith in God's Word. God's Word contains more than seven thousand promises, and when God brings His Word to pass, there is always a harvest or a manifestation of a promise.

One time, a pastor friend of ours named Sam was visiting from Pennsylvania. Sam told me that he came from a Pennsylvania Dutch background, and that he and his eleven brothers and sisters had been raised by strict Mennonite parents. One day, Sam's mother was invited to a Pentecostal church, where she received the baptism of the Holy Spirit. She didn't quite know what to do because her husband was really involved in the Mennonite church, and she knew he would be furious.

I love how godly wisdom leads Spirit-filled people. Sam's mother began praying in tongues every day—but in secret. She prayed for her family, then invited them to attend the Pentecostal church with her. Six of her children were born again and Spirit filled. Later on, those six all graduated from Bible college and went into full-time ministry. How did this happen? Sam's mother walked in faith and godly wisdom, and the results were fantastic! She secured the futures of her children— and the futures of the thousands of people who will be touched by these full-time ministers.

Years later, Sam's father became ill with cancer. However, this man had just gotten ahold of the Word, and he said, "I'm only sixty-five, and it's not time for me to die." God spoke to Sam's father and told him to prophesy and to bless all twelve of his children.

The doctors let him out of the hospital, and all of his children came to see him. They brought their wives and children, and it took two and a half hours for the man to prophesy what God had given him to say to each family member. Sam told me, "Marilyn, our future is secure; we have been blessed by faith by our father."

Similarly, Jacob knew that his future was secure. Why? Because Isaac had blessed him. Despite the trickery Jacob used to receive the blessing, his future was secured when Isaac blessed him by faith. (Certainly, it was not by sight, because Isaac was blind and thought he was blessing Esau instead of Jacob.) This should give us confidence that God will manifest His plans for our lives. Even if we don't have the perfect family, we can secure our future in God's will.

When you look at how Isaac's behavior affected Jacob's life, I want you to notice how the principle of sowing and reaping worked in both their lives. Remember how Isaac's favorite son was Esau, and Rebekah's favorite son was Jacob? Well, Jacob carried on that same behavior—his favorite son was Joseph. *"Now Israel* [Jacob] *loved Joseph more than all his children"* (Genesis 37:3).

Favoritism certainly brought heartaches on Jacob's entire family. Joseph's brothers were jealous of him because of their father's preferential treatment, and they actually hated Joseph because he had a dream about being in a position of authority over them. When he told them about it, *"his brothers said to him, 'Shall you indeed reign over us? Or shall you indeed have dominion over us?' So they hated him even more for his dreams and for his words"* (Genesis 37:8).

Finally, the brothers took Joseph and threw him into a pit. They killed a goat, put its blood on Joseph's special, multicolored coat, took the coat to their father, and told him Joseph had been killed by a wild animal. In reality, they had sold their own brother into slavery. (See Genesis 37:28.)

Did you notice that Jacob's sons deceived their father with a method similar to the one Jacob had used to deceive his father, Isaac? It is too easy to sow wrong things in your future. Jacob sowed some wrong things, and his whole family suffered because he was not walking in godly wisdom.

But Joseph is another success story—he stayed true to God throughout his whole life and became the key to rescuing his family during the great famine. (See Genesis 45:7.) Joseph finally revealed his identity to his brothers and treated them like kings. Joseph had lived his whole life in faith; he walked in great godly wisdom, and he certainly secured a good future for his family.

Joseph's life is a wonderful testimony of how we believers can maintain our faith in God's Word. We can walk in godly wisdom, even when our circumstances fail us. We can Satan-proof our lives by walking in righteousness and holiness. We can pray that our children will never be conformed to the world but will instead transform the world. That's God's wisdom to us. Joseph was a very wise man, and he definitely made a difference in the lives of an entire nation.

> *We can pray that our children will never be conformed to the world but will instead transform the world. That's God's wisdom to us.*

I believe that seeing his son, Joseph, walk in godly wisdom really blessed Jacob, whose name by now had been changed to *Israel*, which means "one who prevails with God and man." And when Israel neared the end of his life, he secured his family's future.

> *Now it came to pass after these things that Joseph was told, "Indeed your father is sick"; and he took with him his two sons, Manasseh and Ephraim....And [Israel] said, "Please bring them to me, and I will bless them."*
> (Genesis 48:1, 9)

But when Israel began to pray for his grandsons, he did something very strange.

> *Then Israel stretched out his right hand and laid it on Ephraim's head, who was the younger, and his left hand on Manasseh's head, guiding his hands knowingly, for Manasseh was the first-born.*
> (Genesis 48:14)

Israel began to bless Joseph's children, saying,

God, before whom my fathers Abraham and Isaac walked, the God who has fed me all my life long to this day...bless the lads; let my name be named upon them, and the name of my fathers Abraham and Isaac; and let them grow into a multitude in the midst of the earth.

(Genesis 48:15–16)

Joseph became a little disturbed when he noticed that his father was giving the firstborn blessing to Ephraim instead of Manasseh, who was the oldest. (See Genesis 48:17–18.) Joseph tried to correct his father, but Israel stood firm in his decision to bless Ephraim.

In studying the history of Ephraim, I found that when he got into the Promised Land, his tribe grew so much that the Ephraimites covered the land more than any other tribe. Manasseh wasn't too far behind him, but Ephraim prospered more. Why? Because Ephraim's future had been secured by Israel, who, in his latter years, began to walk in faith and godly wisdom.

Now, when Joseph neared his death, he said something that long puzzled me: *"Then Joseph took an oath from the children of Israel, saying, 'God will surely visit you, and you shall carry up my bones from here'"* (Genesis 50:25). At one time, I was troubled by this strange request, but God showed me that Joseph knew the Israelites were going to be in Egypt for more than four hundred years. How? Genesis 15 tells us that

Abraham entered into covenant with God, and God said He would deliver Abraham's seed out of Egypt. Abraham shared God's Word with Isaac, Isaac shared God's Word with Jacob, and Jacob shared God's Word with his children. Based on his faith in God and the testimony of God's Word about the Israelites, Joseph had faith for the future of an entire nation. And I want you to know that when the Israelites were delivered from bondage in Egypt, they carried Joseph's bones with them. They carried those bones around in the wilderness for forty years. They didn't have the written Word, but they certainly had the assurance that their future had been secured.

Now, let's review the three types of blessings for your future: material blessings, inheritance, and victory. Just as Abraham blessed Isaac with much of his substance, God wants to bless His people with material blessings. He wants you to prosper. Why? So that you can be a blessing in the kingdom of God. When you sow financial seeds into God's kingdom, you can expect to reap financial blessings in return.

The same thing holds true for prayer. If you will set aside time for prayer each day—not only for yourself, but also for your household—someone will inherit the deposits you are making in your prayer account. And, if you sow prayers, you will reap answers in your own life.

God also wants His people to have faith for future victories. When you begin to Satan-proof your household by walking in faith and godly wisdom, you will get a clearer understanding of the hope that is yours in Jesus Christ, *"who will transform our lowly body that it may be conformed to His glorious body, according to the working by which He is able even to subdue all things to Himself"* (Philippians 3:21).

If the only hope we had was in this life, then we'd all be miserable people. But, when we are born again, our hope is *not* in this life or in our earthly bodies. The Bible says that Jesus is going to raise our bodies and make them like His! So, despite the circumstances around you, get excited, because, through Jesus Christ, God has secured the future for all of His children throughout eternity.

Chapter Eight

Turn on the Light!

Now I want to look at how Satan-proofers can turn on the light wherever there is darkness. You know, at one time, every one of us was in darkness: *"For you were once darkness, but now you are light in the Lord. Walk as children of light"* (Ephesians 5:8).

In this verse, the apostle Paul was exhorting the Christians of Ephesus not to be partakers of the sinful lifestyle from which they had been delivered. The same holds true for us today: sometimes, we try to "measure" the depth of the darkness in which we may have been involved. On our rating scale, we consider some types of darkness to be "greater" than others. Nevertheless, the Word of God warns all of us not to return to the lifestyles in which we were before we accepted Jesus Christ as our Lord and Savior.

BE A LIGHT REFLECTOR

For whom He foreknew, He also predestined to be conformed to the image of His Son.

(Romans 8:29)

When you were born again, God destined you to be conformed into the image of Jesus Christ. An image is a reflection—you are being made into a reflection of Jesus, the Light of the World. (See John 3:19; 9:5.) You aren't the actual Light itself, but you are a *light reflector.* Look at the moon: although it may seem to be a source of light for the planet earth at nighttime, it's actually a mere reflector of light from the sun. As the moon reflects the light of the sun, we believers are to reflect God's Word and His will on the earth. We are destined to be Satan-proofers who shine with the Light of the World.

> *You can Satan-proof your circumstances by allowing God's light to shine forth in your relationships with other people.*

I want you to see how you can walk in God's light and change the circumstances around you. You can Satan-proof your circumstances by allowing God's light to shine forth in your relationships with other people.

When Jesus comes into our hearts and we begin to be conformed into His image, we become instruments God can use to reflect His light—His Word and His will. As we continue to grow in our relationships with the Lord, He will give us more opportunities to reflect His light in the lives of other people. Also, you will often meet other people who "turn on the light" for you. There may come a time when you will be surrounded by the darkness of uncertainty and have a lack of faith. You won't know what to do next about your circumstances, and that's when God will send another believer who will turn on the light for you.

Some years ago, we were trying to get a loan for a new church building. It was a difficult process because, at that time, Denver banks were not loaning money to churches. The building we had moved from hadn't sold right away, and even if it had, the money would not have been nearly enough to meet this new challenge. We had a sort of "rent to own" agreement on the new building, and if we couldn't meet our first month's obligation, the cost of the building would go up by $120,000!

This was a dark time for our ministry. Wally and I were certain that the Lord had led us to acquire a new building, but the finances just didn't seem to be available. Then, one of our church members came up and said, "I believe we can get a loan."

For eight months, this man went from bank to bank trying to get financing. When we would ask him about his progress, he would respond, "No, not yet, but we are going to get a loan!" He kept the light turned on for us. And two weeks before the closing, two banks said yes! We got the loan the day before we would have had to pay the $120,000 increase!

What helped us to get through this stressful period was one of God's *light reflectors*! Our friend was moving in supernatural faith—the faith of Christ—for the situation, and God certainly performed a miracle on our behalf.

How about you? Can you remember a time when you "turned on the light" for someone by standing in faith and praying with that person when his situation looked hopeless? Or, perhaps, you may have been the one who faced a difficult situation that seemed to be beyond your level of faith, and someone else turned on the light for you. Does our loving heavenly Father leave us alone during those stressful periods? No! God will send someone to turn on the light—someone to stand on God's Word with you and pray that His will be done in your life.

The Bible tells how Seth turned on the light after Abel was killed by his brother, Cain. Abel was supposed to be the one to carry the line from Adam and Eve. You could say that, in a sense, Abel was the original seed of promise—the light. Thank God that Adam and Eve had another son, Seth.

> *And Adam knew his wife again, and she bore a son and named him Seth, "For God has appointed another seed for me instead of Abel, whom Cain killed."* (Genesis 4:25)

In the time of Seth's son, Enos, men began to call upon the name of the Lord. Why? Because Seth had been a light reflector—a godly man who had taught his family how to pray. And his family turned on the light for that next generation.

Let me tell you, God will never let His light go out! He will always have men and women whom He can use to manifest His Word and will on the earth. Satan-proofers are just believers who turn on God's light in every situation in which they become involved.

When I think about light reflectors, I can't help thinking about Noah. He lived during a time when it seemed as though God had become fed up with nearly everybody! People were involved in all types of sin. God was so disgusted by all the terrible things people were doing that He was sorry He had ever created man. And He said, *"I will destroy man whom I have created from the face of the earth, both man and beast, creeping thing and birds of the air, for I am sorry that I have made them"* (Genesis 6:7).

It's no wonder that God became fed up! And just when it looked as though it could have been "curtains" for the inhabitants of the earth, Noah found favor with God, and he and his family were spared from destruction. Genesis 6:8 reports, *"But Noah found grace in the eyes of the Lord."*

Out of the entire human race, only Noah and his family allowed themselves to reflect God's Word and His will. Noah loved God and led his family in His ways, and they certainly turned on God's light during that dark period in history.

When you think about becoming a Satan-proofer—someone who turns on God's light in the world—you

> **Just as one candle can light up a dark room, one believer can light up a dark situation.**

might think, *Well, I'm not important; I'm just one person.* However, just as one candle can light up a dark room, one believer can light up a dark situation.

You may be the only person in your family who is a reflector of God's wonderful Word and will. Just hang in there, because if you don't turn on the light for your own loved ones, who will? Even if you become discouraged with them or with yourself, remember that God has placed you there to keep His light turned on in their lives.

One of our care group leaders shared that at one time, he lived with a woman to whom he was not married. Both of them had been brought up in the church, but they had turned their backs on the Lord and had begun to live a worldly lifestyle. One day, God sent a believer who really turned on God's light in that dark situation. The woman was invited to attend one of our church services, and she accepted; meanwhile, the man stayed home to watch football.

At the service, she was born again and Spirit filled, and then she turned on the light in her home. The man she'd been living with also became born again and Spirit filled, and the two of them got married. Today, they have three beautiful children and lead a wonderful ministry in our care groups. The husband recently entered into full-time ministry!

How did this happen? *One person* obeyed God, and God used this believer to turn on His light in this couple's life. I love how God can get so much mileage out of just one believer who is willing to reflect the light of Jesus in the world.

Someone else who reflected God's light was Joseph. He certainly kept God's light turned on for Israel, as well as for Egypt. The nation of Israel was still a small family at this time—just Israel's (Jacob's) household, which was composed of about seventy people. Joseph had been separated from his family ever since his brothers had become jealous and sold him into slavery. Joseph endured terrible hardships and temptations, but he didn't give in to Potiphar's wife when she tried to seduce him, he didn't give in to the pressures of prison, and he didn't give in to bitterness and resentment toward his brothers.

No, Joseph stayed true to God, and God gave him a plan to save Egypt and the whole Middle East area during a tremendous famine. Joseph's family survived because he kept God's light burning. If there ever comes a time when you begin to feel unimportant, just remember Joseph and keep turning on God's light wherever you go. There have been many men like Joseph who allowed themselves to be used by God to turn a particular situation around.

Moses was another one. At first, when God spoke to Moses and told him to get the Israelites delivered out of Egypt, Moses completely blew it. He did everything all wrong and had to go out in the desert to get some more training. For forty years, Moses cared for his father-in-law Jethro's sheep, which certainly was an effective training ground for one who would pastor the entire nation of Israel.

Finally, God commissioned Moses to go down to Egypt and deal with Pharaoh about releasing the Israelites from slavery. Moses and Aaron obeyed God, and they definitely turned on God's light. Through a series of miracles, God began to deal with Pharaoh, and, eventually, the people were set free.

PRAYER TURNS ON GOD'S LIGHT

Moses led the Israelites on what turned out to be a forty-year journey through the wilderness. During this time, Moses had plenty of opportunities to turn on God's light for the Israelites, but those people just murmured and complained much of the time they were in the wilderness—so much so, in fact, that the entire generation, except for Joshua and Caleb, died in the wilderness without ever getting to cross over into the Promised Land.

I think Moses' life gives us insight on how God wants believers to respond when their loved ones seem to want to stay in the darkness of sin. One time, while Moses was up on Mount Sinai to talk with Gold, the people became impatient because they felt that Moses had been gone so long. They told Aaron to make them a golden calf to worship. God said to Moses, "I am so disgusted with them that I want to wipe the whole crowd out and start over with you." (See Exodus 32:10.)

How did Moses respond? He could have said, "Well, God, that's a good idea, because all they do is murmur and whine." But he didn't. Instead, Moses said,

> LORD, why does Your wrath burn hot against Your people whom You have brought out of the land of Egypt with great power and with a mighty hand?...Remember Abraham, Isaac, and Israel, Your servants, to whom You swore by Your own self, and said to them, "I will multiply your descendants as the stars of heaven; and all this land that I have spoken of I give to your descendants, and they shall inherit it forever."
> (Exodus 32:11, 13)

Just as Moses turned on God's light for the children of Israel through prayer, we can pray God's light into one another's circumstances. A while back, we were going through a

> *Just as Moses turned on God's light for the children of Israel through prayer, we can pray God's light into one another's circumstances.*

difficult time with our son, Michael. He had gotten involved with drugs, and he had begun trying to involve
some of the young people of the church in drugs. This
was a dark time for Wally and me. The devil would
taunt us and say things like, "Why are you in the ministry? Even your own child isn't serving God. Who are
you to get up and preach to the people? What is the
church going to say about you? What are people going
to say about you?"

Well, Wally and I just told our members the truth.
We said, "We're having a hard time. Our son is in trouble, and we're in trouble. Will you please pray for us?"
Our congregation members were absolutely fantastic;
they said, "We're going to pray for you, we're going to
fast for you, and we're going to hold on to God's Word
for you." Throughout, I never heard any criticism. Our
congregation kept the light turned on for us.

Another one of my favorite light reflectors from the
Bible is Gideon. I know that we sometimes tend to look
down on Gideon because when the angel first came to
him, Gideon was so pitiful. But the angel saw Gideon
in God's image—as a light reflector—and said to him,
"The Lord is with you, you mighty man of valor!"
(Judges 6:12).

Gideon's response was something like, "Who, me?
Do you know about me? I have a low IQ, and my fam-
ily is poor; we live on the wrong side of the tracks."
Gideon's self-esteem was literally in the pits. But the

angel didn't pay any heed to Gideon's low opinion of himself. He said, "Gideon, you and God can rid the land of the Midianites." (See Judges 6:16.)

Now, during this time, it looked like all of Israel was going to be wiped out by the Midianites, and it certainly didn't look like Gideon was capable of doing anything to stop them. Yet, Gideon continued to listen to God, and God continued to deal with Gideon. Finally, God sent Gideon out to fight the Midianites with only three hundred men. You're probably saying, "Three hundred men against a whole army? They must have had some very powerful weapons!"

You'll be surprised to know that they had only three types of weapons: trumpets, pitchers, and lamps. (See Judges 7:16.) They blew their trumpets and broke their pitchers, and the light from their lamps blazed forth as they shouted, *"The sword of the Lord and of Gideon!"* (Judges 7:20). Then, the Midianites fled and even ended up killing one another with their swords. (See verses 21–22.) Gideon and his little band of soldiers absolutely defeated the fierce Midianite army. How? By carrying God's light.

How often do we allow opportunities for turning on God's light to slip away because we are afraid? Some of you look at yourselves and think, *I've never attended Bible school; I didn't graduate from high school; I don't have any experience; I'm not good looking; I say the wrong things; I just can't do it!*

That is a lie from the devil because you can do all things through Christ, who strengthens you. (See Philippians 4:13.) Despite your shortcomings and faults, God can use you to turn on His light in the circumstances around you. Look at all the men I have mentioned. They were willing to listen to God, and as they began to respond, He used them to turn their situations around.

It's a tremendous blessing to be able to turn on His light in a dark situation. It's also a blessing when God sends someone else to turn on the light for you. One time, about seven or eight years ago, I had the feeling that some of my staff members were just going to quit the ministry because they thought I had made some wrong decisions. One young woman came to me crying, and I thought she was about to say that she quit. So, I asked her, "Are you going to quit?" She said, "Quit? No! God called me here, and although I may not understand everything you do, I have confidence in you." Folks, her encouragement meant so much to me; it was as if she had turned the light back on for me.

Turning on God's light doesn't always have to be some big thing. For the most part, God's light will shine in the little things that we do.

We won't always be aware when we have turned on the light for someone. That's why we must be so cautious to be led by the Holy Spirit in our dealings with other people. Sometimes, God's loving light may shine through someone else's darkness because of your smile, your prayers, or your kind words. Turning on God's light doesn't always have to be some big thing. For the most part, God's light will shine in the little things that we do.

I read an interesting description about a glowworm. The steps it takes are so small, they can hardly be measured. And, as the glowworm moves across a field at midnight, it produces just enough light in its glow to illuminate one single step forward. So, as the glowworm moves ahead, it always moves into light.

Sometimes, God will allow you to bless others in a way that will produce obvious results in their lives. But, more often, God will allow you to be like the glowworm—you'll turn His light on during someone's dark moments or moods, and, little by little, that person will begin to move into God's direction for his life.

AN UNEXPECTED LIGHT REFLECTOR

You know, sometimes, God's light may be turned on by the most unexpected people, such as happened to the child Samuel. He came on the scene during a very pitiful situation. Samuel probably expected Eli to be the one who would turn on the light. After all, Eli was the high priest who was supposed to instruct Samuel in the priesthood. But, sadly, Eli was not obedient to God's instructions concerning childrearing. Eli had two sons, Hophni, and Phinehas, whom he had so indulged that he hadn't disciplined or trained them. They were involved in adultery, and they were stealing from the sacrifice offerings. (See 1 Samuel 2:12–16, 22.)

It certainly looked like God's light for Israel's spiritual atmosphere was about to go out. However, instead of Eli turning on the light for Israel, Samuel was God's man for the occasion.

Even when Samuel was a young boy, God talked to him, and Samuel began to hear God's voice. (See 1 Samuel 3:4–14.) Samuel didn't become rebellious toward Eli and say, "You're a poor example to me; how can I be a believer? And look at your kids—they're the pits." No, Samuel kept holding on to God's Word.

Later, when Israel was attacked by the Philistines (see 1 Samuel 4:1), the ark of the covenant was taken, and both of Eli's sons were killed in battle. When Eli heard the news, he *fell off the seat backward by the side of the gate; and his neck was broken and he died, for the man was old and heavy. And he had judged Israel forty years"* (1 Samuel 4:18).

Phinehas' pregnant wife went into labor when the news came. Evidently, she was not in good health because when her son was born, she was near death.

> *The women who stood by her said to her, "Do not fear, for you have borne a son." But she did not answer, nor did she regard it. Then she named the child Ichabod, saying, "The glory has departed from Israel!"* (1 Samuel 4:20–21)

She thought that God's light had been turned off, but she was wrong. The glory of God hadn't departed from Israel. Do you know why? Because Samuel had God's light inside of him.

It doesn't matter who blows it or backslides; that is not our problem. A Satan-proofer will keep God's light on. Jesus is the light, and He is inside every believer. If we will stand in His light, who knows what we can do for those who backslide or blow it?

A woman called in one day with a praise report. Previously, she had requested prayer because her son's girlfriend was pregnant and was scheduled to have an abortion. However, a Christian friend prayed with the young woman and helped her to understand that abortion was wrong. Praise God, the young woman changed her mind and decided to keep her baby.

I don't know whether this young woman has received Christ or not, but I do know that her Christian friend turned on God's light in her dark situation. And I believe that the woman's son, his girlfriend, and the baby are all going to become born again and Spirit filled.

Folks, when we pray for each other, we are turning on God's light. I love to turn on God's light for other people. Don't you? Wouldn't you rather pray and bring forth God's Word and will in people's lives than to turn off God's light by participating in gossip and strife? Well, evidently, Samuel chose to keep the light on for Israel, and the nation didn't go under, because God's light was shining through him.

When I'm traveling, people sometimes come to me with all kinds of stories about troublesome leadership in their churches. I always challenge them to be Satan-proofers. I ask them, "Well, are you standing in faith? Are you praying? Or are you criticizing and being negative?" I think that God sometimes allows us to see problems so that we can pray and keep His light turned on until He turns the situation around.

> *I think that God sometimes allows us to see problems so that we can pray and keep His light turned on until He turns the situation around.*

Another place where I have seen people turn on God's light is in marriages that look like they are falling apart. One spouse may keep God's light burning, and many of those marriages are standing strong today. Why? Because one believing spouse refused to let God's light go out in his or her marriage.

There was another time in Israel's history when it looked like the light of God's spiritual atmosphere was about to go out. A king named Jehoram had married a wicked woman named Athaliah—in my opinion, she is the worst woman in the Bible. You may be thinking, *No, Jezebel was the worst*. Well, Athaliah was Jezebel's daughter, and I think that Athaliah was much better at being evil than Jezebel.

After Athaliah's husband died, their son, Ahaziah, took the throne of Judah and was killed while visiting the king of Israel. Athaliah wanted the throne so much that she ordered the murder of her own grandchildren. (See 2 Kings 11:1.) This woman certainly was the pits! Her actions could have eliminated all hope for the Messiah to come forth from the house of David. This would have been absolutely devastating for Israel, as well as for you, me, and the rest of the body of Christ!

But God had a provision for this critical situation. His provision came in the form of a priest named Jehoiada, who had married Athaliah's daughter, Jehosheba. When her mother began to murder all the children, Jehosheba slipped in, took the only remaining grandchild, Joash, and hid him from his wicked grandmother. (See 2 Kings 11:2.) I really admire Jehosheba's courage and her desire to do God's will, even though it meant going against her mother, who was quite capable of killing Jehosheba.

But Jehosheba probably said something like, "God will take care of me. If I perish, I perish, but the light cannot go out for the house of David." So, she stole that tiny baby and hid him in her home for six years. She and Jehoiada raised Joash, and when he was seven years old, they secretly took him into the temple to be crowned the rightful king of Israel. (See 2 Kings 11:11–12.)

In the midst of the celebration, Athaliah burst in and interrupted everything. *"When Athaliah heard the noise of the escorts and the people, she came to the people in the temple of the Lord....All the people of the land were rejoicing and blowing trumpets. So Athaliah tore her clothes and cried out, 'Treason! Treason!'"* (verses 13–14).

But her cries were in vain:

Jehoiada the priest commanded the captains of the hundreds, the officers of the army, and said to them, "Take her outside under guard, and slay with the sword whoever follows her." For the priest had said, "Do not let her be killed in the house of the LORD." So they seized her; and she went by way of the horses' entrance into the king's house, and there she was killed. (verses 15–16)

Folks, despite all the devil's attempts, God's light will never go out! He will always have men and women—Satan-proofers—who will say, "God, I am going to stay true to You and turn Your light on in this situation."

I'll give you another example of someone who reflected God's will—Daniel. While Daniel was enslaved in Babylon, he turned on God's light for three kings: Nebuchadnezzar, Belshazzar, and Darius. Daniel had favor with God in the area of interpreting dreams and visions. Now, he could have sold out and turned away from God's people; after all, they had been taken into captivity because of their own sin. But Daniel stayed true to God and to His people, and he prayed for the Jews.

Then, one night, something strange happened while King Belshazzar was having a big drunken party: *"In the same hour the fingers of a man's hand appeared and wrote opposite the lampstand on the plaster of the wall of the king's palace"* (Daniel 5:5).

Can you imagine how unusual that must have been? Suddenly, a hand appeared out of nowhere and began to write on the wall. Well, Belshazzar was terrified:

Then the king's countenance changed, and his thoughts troubled him, so that the joints of his hips were loosened and his knees knocked against each other. (verse 6)

I think it's almost funny! Here, Belshazzar was making a mockery out of God by allowing the golden vessels that had been taken out of the temple to be used as drinking glasses at this party. But what happened when the hand of God appeared? Belshazzar's face became pale, his whole body began to tremble, and his knees started knocking!

None of the king's astrologers or soothsayers knew what had been written on the wall or what it meant. In fact, there was only one person in the entire kingdom who could interpret the handwriting on the wall. That's right—Daniel was the only man who could turn on God's light in that situation.

When you look around you and see all the trouble in the world, don't get nervous, because it can't be that dark if you're around. You are a Satan-proofer.

Folks, when you look around you and see all the trouble in the world, don't get nervous, because it can't be that dark if you're around. You are a Satan-proofer—God's provision for dark situations. All you have to do is to turn on God's light wherever you go.

The last person I want to tell you about is the apostle Paul, whose name was originally Saul.

> *As he journeyed he came near Damascus, and suddenly a light shone around him from heaven. Then he fell to the ground, and heard a voice saying to him, "Saul, Saul, why are you persecuting Me?"* (Acts 9:3–4)

Before Saul met Jesus, he was in darkness. Even though he may have loved God, he was trying to serve God with his mind and his legalistic teaching. However, God wanted Paul to turn on His light, and so God sent the light—Jesus—to Saul. After Saul received the light of Christ, God made him a light to the Gentiles. (See Acts 13:47.) God sent Paul to preach to the Gentiles, and that was the beginning of a tremendous revival that would extend all the way down to you and me.

Just as Paul was a light reflector, you and I are light reflectors, too. Jesus is the Light of the World, and although we believers are not the actual light itself, we are to reflect the Word and will of the marvelous light who dwells inside us. Through the power of God, we can be Satan-proofers as we reflect God's Word and will throughout the earth.

Chapter Nine

Getting God's Priorities

If I were to ask you what you thought God's number one priority was, would you answer, "People"? If so, you'd be exactly right—God is just wild over people! We are His number one priority. The Bible says that when God created people, *"God blessed them, and God said to them, 'Be fruitful and multiply; fill the earth'"* (Genesis 1:28).

This Scripture lets us know that God loved people so much that He wasn't satisfied with just one couple; rather, He wanted the earth to be inhabited with lots and lots of people. So, He told Adam and Eve, "I want you to go forth, bring forth fruit—to have children—and replenish the earth." Notice how God refers to people as *"fruit."* I guess we could say that God's favorite fruit are His children: *"Behold, children are a heritage from the Lord, the fruit of the womb is a reward"* (Psalm 127:3).

Here, again, we see the great importance God places upon children. Those of you who don't have children may ask, "How does this teaching apply to me?" It applies to you because, someday, if you get married and have children, you'll need to know how to Satan-proof your children through proper parenting. I believe that if you begin to plan ahead and learn now, God will give you so much wisdom about parenting that, by the time you do have children, you'll be one of the absolute best parents in the world!

God says that children are our heritage, our fruit, our reward. I imagine that there are plenty of times when some parents feel like they could have done without some of their reward. Nevertheless, God says that children are our heritage. God places a priority on the family, and He considers our children to be extremely important.

GOD'S FIRSTFRUITS

I want to talk to you about firstfruits. When you see the word "firstfruits" in the Bible, it's identifying God's priorities. Needless to say, God's firstfruits—His priorities—may not always be the same as ours, even though they should be. What are God's firstfruits?

God told the Israelites that their firstfruits—their firstborn male children—belonged to Him. However, instead of literally taking their sons away from them, God designated the entire tribe of Levites to symbolize the firstfruits of the nation of Israel: *"And you shall take the Levites for Me; I am the Lord; instead of all the firstborn among the children of Israel"* (Numbers 3:41).

The Israelites participated in dedication ceremonies for their children—on the thirtieth day after the first male child was born in a family, the mother and father would present their baby to the priest, who would ask the mother, "Is this your firstborn son?" She would say, "Yes, it is." Then, the priest would ask the father, "Is this your firstborn son?" and the father would respond, "Yes, it is." By affirming the child to be their firstborn, these parents were symbolically giving the child to God.

Next, the parents would be required to redeem their child—buy him back—by paying the priest five shekels (about $3.20). (See Numbers 3:40–51.) You may think it pretty strange that parents had to buy back their own children—and for only $3.20 apiece! Actually, this amount was a tax that God had imposed to provide financial support for the priests and Levites.

However, the concept of redemption is extremely important to you and me today because we, as believers, have been redeemed: *"Christ has redeemed us from the curse of the law"* (Galatians 3:13). We have not been redeemed with corruptible things like silver and gold, but with the precious blood of Jesus. (See 1 Peter 1:18; Revelation 5:9.) Since God has destined all people to come into His family, every person born on this earth is a potential firstborn child of God. Do you see how people are God's number one priority?

People aren't God's only firstfruits. God also talked to the Israelites about the firstfruits of their harvest. (See Exodus 23:16.) God said, "Make Me your priority. Put Me first in whatever you do. At the beginning of the harvest, bring Me your firstfruits." Today, you give God the firstfruits of your harvest when you pay your tithes—10 percent of your income—to the storehouse (your local church). By doing this, you are saying, "God, You are the priority in my life. You are my Source, and I am returning my firstfruits to You."

God has commanded His people to tithe, saying, *"Bring all the tithes into the storehouse"* (Malachi 3:10). It's too bad that many Christians allow God to deliver them from all sorts of sinful lifestyles, attend church regularly, and study their Bibles, but are not committed tithers. Then, they wonder why they never seem to be able to accomplish their financial goals. It's because they do not trust God to Satan-proof their finances by tithing their firstfruits. They ignore the assurance in Malachi 3:11: *"And I will rebuke the devourer for your sakes, so that he will not destroy the fruit of your ground."*

I have noticed that people who faithfully pay their tithes seem to have much more than people who don't. I have also heard some amazing testimonies of how God has taken 90 percent of someone's income and stretched it to meet every financial need—and with some left over! When Christians tell me about their financial problems, I always ask them, "Do you tithe?" Some people respond, "No, I can't afford it." I tell them, "You really can't afford *not* to tithe."

Folks, whether we like it or not, we have to obey God, and He has said that our tithes—our firstfruits— belong to Him. When we give God our firstfruits, it's as if we are planting a seed. God will multiply that seed and bring forth a great harvest.

Another one of God's first-fruits is the nation of Israel: *"Israel was holiness to the Lord, the firstfruits of His increase. All that devour him will offend; disaster will come upon them,' says the Lord"* (Jeremiah 2:3). God claimed the whole nation of Israel as

> **When we give God our firstfruits, it's as if we are planting a seed. God will multiply that seed and bring forth a great harvest.**

His, and whenever God talks about His "firsts," He is planning on a big harvest. So, although Israel may have been God's first nation, just look at the millions of people from other nations who were born again because of God's dealings with the Israelites!

Israel was the seed from which God expected a great harvest of many other nations to become His people. The same principle will work for us today concerning our children. When we dedicate our children to God as infants and bring them up in the fear and admonition of the Lord, what happens? God becomes their priority, and they begin to witness to others about the love of Jesus Christ. They begin to turn on God's light in other people's lives and bring others to Christ!

Have you ever heard people say, "You can't out-give God"? That certainly is true; as God said, "Because people are My priority and I am asking them to give to

Me their firstfruits, I am going to give back to them My best—My firstborn Son." Who is God's firstborn Son? Yes, it's Jesus.

> *For whom [God] foreknew, He also predestined to be conformed to the image of His Son, that He might be the firstborn among many brethren.*
> (Romans 8:29)

> *In [Jesus] we have redemption through His blood, the forgiveness of sins. He is the image of the invisible God, the firstborn over all creation.*
> (Colossians 1:14–15)

> *But when [God] again brings the firstborn into the world, He says: "Let all the angels of God worship Him."*
> (Hebrews 1:6)

God gave us His firstborn, Jesus, because He wanted a harvest—a great, big family of *"joint heirs"* with Christ.

> *The Spirit Himself bears witness with our spirit that we are children of God, and if children, then heirs; heirs of God and joint heirs with Christ.*
> (Romans 8:16–17)

God invites all of us to come into His kingdom as heirs—indeed, coheirs with Jesus Christ. God's number one priority is people. We have always been God's first concern.

CARING FOR GOD'S PRIORITIES

When we look at how God taught the Israelites to take care of their children, we see the image of what kind of parents God wants us to be and how He wants our children to be our priorities.

Remember that in Chapter 5, we discussed how all people are destined—set apart—to subdue the earth and to be blessed—to be put in an attitude of worship. This can take place only after our minds have been renewed, and we have been conformed into the image of Jesus Christ. Right? Therefore, it's when we become born again that we become God's firstborn.

I really want you to understand that you must be born again. Just because your parents may be born-again Christians does not automatically mean that you are a Christian. No, you have to receive Christ into your life. Your parents may stand in faith for your salvation, but you personally have to be born again.

When you are born again, you become a firstborn, because Jesus is God's firstborn, and you came into God's family through your faith in Christ. Now look at what Jesus says about you: *"And I have declared to them Your [God's] name, and will declare it, that the love with which You loved Me may be in them, and I in them"* (John 17:26).

199

Jesus said that His heavenly Father loves you just as much as He loves Jesus. I know that it sounds too wonderful to be true; nonetheless, God loves you just as much as He loves Jesus.

PROTECTING GOD'S PRIORITIES

Let's look back and see what God said about the Egyptians' firstborn when the Israelites were captives of Pharaoh: "I am going to judge Egypt; I am going to send the devourer and take the firstborn child and firstborn of every animal in Egypt!" (See Exodus 11:4–6.) God had already destroyed the first part of their harvest.

It must have been truly devastating for the Egyptians to have all their firstborn children, animals, and possessions destroyed. They probably wondered why the Israelites weren't experiencing the same catastrophes. It's because the Israelites were under God's protection, and they obeyed God's Word, which directed them thusly:

> *On the tenth day of this month every man shall take for himself a lamb, according to the house of his father, a lamb for a household....Your lamb shall be without blemish, a male of the first year. You may take it from the sheep or from the goats. Now you shall keep it until the fourteenth day of the same month. Then the whole assembly of*

*the congregation of Israel shall kill it at twilight.
And they shall take some of the blood and put
it on the two doorposts and on the lintel of the
houses where they eat it.* (Exodus 12:3, 5–7)

The essence of the message was that every house
with the blood of a sacrificial lamb on its doorpost would
be passed over by the death angel, who would see the
blood; the firstborn of every house would be protected
under the blood covenant. During the Passover, God
wanted to save the adult Israelites from destruction,
but He also wanted to save their children.

The same thing holds true
today. It's not enough for us
adults to be saved; God wants
our children to be under His
blood covenant and to become
His firstborn through Jesus
Christ. Children are our fruit,
our reward, and our heritage,
and it is extremely important to
God that our children be born
into His kingdom. That's why
God told the Israelites to put

> *Children are
> our fruit, our
> reward, and our
> heritage, and
> it is extremely
> important to
> God that our
> children be
> born into His
> kingdom.*

the blood on the doorposts—so that their children could
become a part of the covenant relationship with God.

Now, you may be saying, "Yes, Marilyn, but you just
said that parents can't make the decision concerning
salvation for their children." You're right; however, let

me show you what parents can do. After our relationships with God and our relationships with our spouses, we can make our relationships with our children our first priority. While children are living in our homes, they come under our protective covenant with God: *"For the unbelieving husband is sanctified by the wife, and the unbelieving wife is sanctified by the husband; otherwise your children would be unclean, but now they are holy"* (1 Corinthians 7:14).

Did you realize that one believer in the household causes the blood of Jesus to be over that entire household? That's right! The blood of Jesus in one believer sanctifies the home and marks—sets apart, or calls God's attention to—every person living in that household. God is not interested only in that one believer; He also wants to establish a covenant relationship with every member of the family. God wants us, as Christian parents, to bring forth our fruit (our children) so that they can replenish the earth.

Let's compare Scripture with Scripture and see what Jesus said about your fruit: *"I have...appointed you that you should go and bear fruit, and that your fruit should remain"* (John 15:16).

Now, look back at Genesis 1:28, where God told Adam and Eve to be fruitful. Then, turn to Psalm 127:3–5, which says that children are your fruit because they are your inheritance and reward. When you bring forth children into the world, and then into God's kingdom, they can be blessed (brought into an attitude of worship). Then, they will begin to Satan-proof the earth by becoming light reflectors. They will reflect God's wonderful Word and will into the dark places in other people's lives and cause them to come closer to God.

That's why God doesn't want us parents to be nonchalant when it comes to taking care of our children. We can't just casually give them a Bible and tell them to read it when they get older or if they feel like it. We can't treat our children like that and expect them to be the fruit that remains. God doesn't want our children or grandchildren to be lost; He wants us to take our

> *God doesn't want our children or grandchildren to be lost; He wants us to take our fruit to heaven with us.*

fruit to heaven with us. And, since our children are God's number one priority, we parents need to be sure that our children are a number one priority for us, too.

GOD'S PRIORITIES VERSUS WORLD PR

There is so much emphasis that it's no wonder we refer to tural tides as the "rat race." So so involved in getting ahead

his became humiliation

they have begun to neglect their children. For instance, when both parents work, it is not uncommon for them to work so hard that they have little time to spend with their children. When this happens, what do they do? They purchase a big TV with hundreds of channels or buy video games for their children, then worry about their children's being exposed to too much violence.

I am not saying that parents shouldn't work, but I am saying that many parents have set their priorities in the wrong places. Too many parents work themselves to the point where they come home feeling too tired to spend time with their children. They try to squeeze all their children's "time needs" into a tight, little box that we call "quality time," but, sadly, their children are going down the drain because they receive such a low priority in their parents' lives. Yet, God says that our children are our reward, our heritage, and our fruit. They are fruit that is to remain after we leave the earth.

I received a testimony from a woman whose father's distorted sense of priorities caused tremendous suffering for his entire family. This man was unable to find employment, and instead of seeking God's provision for his family, he made the decision to become involved in organized crime. How tragic! Instead of protecting family and Satan-proofing his household, this man the tool through which Satan brought terrible and torment to his entire family.

Why did this family suffer? Because the father's priorities were out of order. Remember, after our relationships with God and then with our spouses, our children come first. If this father had been seeking God's wisdom for himself first and then for his family, this tragedy never would have occurred.

Let's talk about some other things that are wrong to prioritize, such as cars, houses, and jobs. Again, I am not saying that it is wrong to desire these things, but that some parents—fathers, especially—often place more emphasis on paying for a new car than playing with their children. When Jesus returns to rapture the body of Christ, are they going to say, "Please, let me take my Porsche with me"? They may say it, but, believe me, their cars are staying here!

What about a new house? So what if it does have five bedrooms and four baths—if the owner is a believer, after Jesus comes, someone else will be enjoying the house, and its former occupant will be gone.

And consider someone with a prestigious position he thinks highly of—maybe he's the president or CEO of a company. He can't take his position to heaven with him, but he can take his children with him. Next to God and his spouse, they are the most precious part of his life. They are a number one priority with God, and they need to be a number one priority with him, too.

TAKE YOUR CHILDREN TO HEAVEN WITH YOU

There are four important principles I want to share with you about taking your children to heaven with you: how to view them as God views them, how to teach them, how to pray with them, and how to model holy living for them.

View Your Children as God Views Them

Some of you may be thinking, *Marilyn, I'd like to take my children with me to heaven. I've tried to talk with them about it, but they are just not responding.* Regardless of what the circumstances may look like, your children can go with you to heaven. The first thing to do is learn to see your children as God sees them—as precious and valuable. Begin to think of your children as beautiful fruit whom you will prepare to carry the love of Christ.

Let me share with you a testimony about a young man whose family did not understand that he was a number one priority with God. At a very young age, this boy was sexually abused by his grandmother and mentally and physically abused by his parents.

After his parents' divorce, the boy's mother got a job, and he became a latchkey kid. The mother wrote that her son had been so deeply wounded by all the abuse he had suffered that he tried to do everything he could not be a burden upon her. He took care of the house while his mother worked, he was never late for school, and he was never in any trouble. He lived silently within himself to the point where he never shared with his mother his needs concerning school or anything else. His mother did not see her son as a priority; instead, she focused all her attention on herself.

This boy's parents may have ignored their fruit, but the devil certainly didn't. By the time the boy was in sixth grade, he began to change and started drinking, smoking, and taking drugs. However, his mother's life began to change, as well. She remarried a man who also became a negative force in her son's life, but she also rededicated herself to God and became Spirit filled.

The mother started praying for her son, and God began to reveal how the abusive behavior had shaped his life. The Holy Spirit instructed her how to be loving, supportive, and understanding—how to become the protector of her fruit, even when it meant taking a stand against the abusive behavior of her new husband. She wrote:

> One gift that God has given me is the steadfast determination to follow through once I know I have heard from Him. I have watched my son go from being unloved, abused, and having a terrible chip on his shoulder, to becoming softened

and opened to me again. His "I love ya, Mom" is more precious than anything else I have ever accomplished with God's help.

Although this family's circumstances may be far from ideal, God is definitely moving in a powerful way to bring forth His desires in the mother's life and in the life of one of His number one priorities—her child.

Often, when our children are being particularly sweet, we think, *Oh, aren't they a beautiful reward?* When our children aren't being so sweet, however, we say, "I can't deal with them; they're too hard to handle." Yet, God didn't say our children are our reward only when they are well-behaved and nice, did He? No, He said they are our reward, period! No matter how they act, our children are still our inheritance.

It's so important for us to understand that even when we may have blown it with our children and they become difficult to deal with, our children are still our fruit. When we parents begin to trust God and line our lives up with His Word and will, pretty soon, we'll begin to see our children become the precious, valuable fruit that God sees when He looks at them.

Teach Your Children

Another thing we Christian parents need to do is to teach God's Word and His principles to our children. Some of you think that bringing your children to Sunday school once a week is enough. But, folks, forty-five minutes or an hour per week simply is not enough time for your children to spend learning about God.

The book of Deuteronomy contains the most intense teaching program for children that I know of:

You shall teach them to your children, speaking of them when you sit in your house, when you walk by the way, when you lie down, and when you rise up. And you shall write them on the doorposts of your house and on your gates, that your days and the days of your children may be multiplied in the land of which the LORD swore to your fathers to give them, like the days of the heavens above the earth.

(Deuteronomy 11:19–21)

God puts the responsibility for teaching our children about Him squarely on our shoulders! Let me ask you, do you read the Bible with your children? Do you help them apply God's Word to their everyday situations? If you want to please God concerning your children, then give Him reason to say of you what He said of Abraham: "*For I have known him, in order that he may command his children and his household after him, that they keep the way of the Lord*" (Genesis 18:19).

Christians are the seed of Abraham. What did God say about Abraham's seed? He said that He would bless and multiply them. (See Genesis 22:17.) Friends, God wants to bless and multiply us, and He wants to bless

> **God wants to bless and multiply us, and He wants to bless and multiply our seed.**

and multiply our seed. But, like Abraham, we must understand that this blessing won't happen automatically, just because our children were born into our households. No, our children will be blessed and multiplied when we do your part and *teach* them in the ways of the Lord.

Begin to Satan-proof your children by applying the blood of Jesus to their lives, by seeing them as valuable individuals, and by teaching them God's Word. Then, when they are old enough, they will make the same wise decision to receive our loving Savior into their hearts that you did.

When my son, Mike, was about ten or eleven years old, I began to memorize the book of Proverbs. I thought that it would be good if my children memorized some of it, too, so I had Mike and Sarah memorize the first six chapters of Proverbs.

One day, Mike said, "Mother, I have talked with the kids at church, and you're the only mother who makes her children memorize Proverbs." I didn't respond, so he became more dramatic. "You know, Mother, you're probably the only mother in the whole city who makes her children memorize Proverbs." When I still didn't respond, Mike became a little desperate. "Mother! This is horrible; you're the only mother in the whole wide *world* who makes her children memorize Proverbs!" I finally said, "I think that's wonderful, Mike. You are so blessed to have the only mother in the world who is helping you to memorize God's Word."

The Bible says that if we raise our children in the ways of God, then when they are old, they will not depart from those ways. (See Proverbs 22:6.) Even now, when Mike visits me at my office, he often will encourage me with some of the Scriptures he memorized as a child. When you begin to plant God's Word into your children's hearts and minds, remember that the Word cannot return void. (See Isaiah 55:11.) God's Word will always prosper and accomplish the work that God has set forth for it to do in your children's lives.

Pray Daily for Your Children

The third important point is daily prayer. Wally and I always supported our children in their school activities. One day, at one of Sarah's basketball games, the woman sitting next to me shared that she and her husband had been born again and were Spirit filled. However, when they'd shared the good news of their conversion with their two teenage daughters, the daughters had become very upset. They'd begun griping and complaining because their parents would pray and quote Scriptures at mealtimes. The daughters would say, "We're so tired of all this 'Amen' and 'Hallelujah' stuff!" They had been really resistant to their parents' new lifestyle, and there had been a lot of strife within the home.

So, the woman had begun to pray, asking God to give her wisdom in the situation. The Lord told her to fast one day each week and to pray for her children, and she did that for seven months. Now, both of her daughters are born again and Spirit filled, and they regularly join their mother and father in praising the Lord.

Pray for your children on a regular basis, and don't forget to pray with them. I often hear parents talk about how much time they spend praying *for* their children, but they neglect to pray *with* them. Along with teaching our children the Word of God, we need to teach them how to pray fervently, for "*the effective, fervent prayer of a righteous man avails much*" (James 5:16).

Again, the word *fervent* can mean "very hot, glowing." Make sure that your children know how to pray those glowing, white-hot prayers that really get things moving in the spirit realm.

Let's look at another truth about prayer. One morning, I was praying for my son, and the Lord spoke to my heart, "Marilyn, you're going to get your reward in your children." When I asked God how this would happen, He impressed upon me Hebrews 11:6: "*For he who comes to God must believe that He is, and that He is a rewarder of those who diligently seek Him*" (Hebrews 11:6).

When we "*diligently seek*" God concerning our children, we will see our children as our reward. So, start praying for your children right now. Pray for their education, for their friends, and for their future spouses. Start Satan-proofing their futures. In the name of

Jesus, claim that your children are going to heaven with you—even if you have to drag them by their heels!

When we "diligently seek" God concerning our children, we will see our children as our reward.

Begin daily vigils over your children. Rebuke the devil and, in Jesus' name, refuse to let him have your seed! Determine to pray your children into heaven, and, even if it happens the last second before they die, they will receive Jesus into their hearts.

Model Holy Living for Your Children

Lastly, I want to talk about your lifestyle. You simply cannot live a double standard before your children. You can't tell your children, "I don't want you to drink, smoke, take drugs, or become sexually active" unless you yourself are living a clean life and eschewing those behaviors. They'll think of you as a hypocrite, and they'll be right. If you live a sloppy life, then you can't expect your children to prosper because you're sowing bad seed into their lives.

One woman told me that she really wanted her daughter to be born again and to commit herself totally to Jesus Christ. Now, this mother was a Christian, but she was haphazard in her church attendance and didn't tithe. I'm going to tell you something—your children will reap the type of life that you sow. Your children will follow your example.

Again, the Bible says that one believer sanctifies the family. If you're not conducting your life according to God's Word, then don't expect your children to live consecrated lives, either.

Before we go any further, I would like for you to pray with me:

Dear heavenly Father, I thank You today for Your wonderful Word and its assurance for my children. Thank You for my rewards, my inheritance—for this marvelous fruit that You have put in my hands. Now, Father, I lift up those areas where I have failed, and I repent of my sins and shortcomings. From now on, after my relationship with You and my spouse, I commit my children to be my number one priority. I promise to view them as valuable individuals, to teach them Your Word (if I cannot share it with them personally, I will mail them each a Bible), to pray for them, and to lead a holy life before them. When I go to heaven, I know that my children will be following me. In Jesus' name, amen.

Chapter Ten

Transforming Power

I am sure that you all want to see your families go forward; you want to see your spouses, your children, and the rest of your loved ones really begin to walk victoriously in the Lord. So, when your loved ones are suffering, wounded, or defeated, it hurts you, too, doesn't it?

I remember the first time my daughter, Sarah, had a high temperature. She was only about three months old, and we were planning a trip to Nebraska. She was so sick, and although we prayed and prayed, she didn't seem to be getting any better. In fact, she got worse. Finally, Wally said, "I'm going to go to the drugstore to get something for her. Call the doctor; we just can't go on like this."

To see our helpless little baby suffering was so difficult for us. I know that most of you have felt (or will feel) the same way at some point. It hurts to see our loved ones suffer. It also hurts when we know that our loved ones are not walking in the victory available for them in Jesus Christ. However, as Satan-proofers, we are not going to focus upon the hurts; we are going to focus on Jesus Christ! By faith, we are going to take authority over our loved ones' situations and begin to operate in God's transforming power for them. That is the purpose of a Satan-proofer—to transform the circumstances and subdue the earth.

God never intended for us to stand by passively and watch the devil cover the earth with destruction. That's why God gave believers authority over the devil: *"Behold, I give unto you* **power** *to tread on serpents and scorpions, and over all the* **power** *of the enemy: and nothing shall by any means hurt you"* (Luke 10:19 KJV, emphasis added).

> **You received God's authority the moment you were born again, and if you have been baptized in the Holy Spirit, you have been given God's miracle-working power.**

In Chapter 6, we saw that the first time the word *"power"* appears in this verse, it refers to "authority"; the second time, it refers to "miracle-working power." You received God's authority the moment you were born again, and if you have been baptized in the Holy Spirit, you have been given God's miracle-working power. What are you supposed to do with God's authority and power? Stop Satan from wreaking havoc in your area of influence.

There was a woman from Chicago who had been participating in our Bible-reading plan, and she wrote to us to say that her son had been classified by the police as a habitual criminal—he was hopelessly locked in a criminal mind-set. But, praise God—as this woman began to feed on God's Word, it began to change her from being hopeless to being hopeful about her son. Proverbs 11:21 says, *"Though they join forces, the wicked will not go unpunished; but the posterity of the righteous will be delivered."*

This woman had gotten ahold of God's Word concerning a promise for her son. She began to Satan-proof her child and reminded God of His Word, saying, "Father, You promised me that my seed will be delivered." Let me tell you, folks, God's Word is *transforming power*, and it absolutely reversed the course of her son's life.

This diligent mother stood on Proverbs 11:21. She began to meditate on it, speak it aloud, and pray it. During the testimony service at her church, she boldly proclaimed, "I know God is going to save my son, and he will preach the gospel in this church."

Of course, the other members probably thought, *You poor, deluded woman. Your son is always going to be the pits.* Yet, she told me, "Marilyn, I didn't let the dirty looks affect me; I just held on to God's Word." She had focused all her attention on God's Word—His *transforming power.*

One night, at ten o'clock, she felt an unusual burden to pray in tongues for her son. He called her long-distance an hour later, asking what she had been doing between ten and ten-thirty that night. He had sold some bad drugs to a man who had come to his apartment during that time and beat him to a pulp. The man had pulled out a gun, intending to shoot my friend's son, but whenever he'd tried to pull the trigger, his finger had not been able to bend! He'd tried several times but just hadn't been able to do it. Finally, he'd thrown the gun down and run out, saying, "Your mother is doing something to stop me from pulling this trigger!" Imagine, this gunman knew that his intended victim's mother was stopping him from killing her son!

She had been praying God's Word for her son— *God's transforming power.* When her son came home, he was born again and filled with the Spirit. He began attending Bible school and was soon invited to be a guest speaker at their church.

> **God's will is His Word. It is His transforming power, and it can have tremendous impact in your life, as well as in the lives of your loved ones.**

You see, your loved ones can be transformed! If they are living lives filled with hopelessness and despair, then it's because they are living outside of God's will. God's will is His Word. It is His *transforming power*, and it can have tremendous impact in your life, as well as in the lives of your loved ones.

I am going to give you five things to consider as you begin to Satan-proof your household through God's *transforming power*: the father's faith; it's time for our loved ones to arise; the mother's faith; power to transform the past; and catching the faith vision for your loved ones.

THE FATHER'S FAITH

We're going to look first at the faith of fathers: "*So Jesus came again to Cana of Galilee where He had made the water wine. And there was a certain nobleman whose son was sick at Capernaum*" (John 4:46). This man was a Gentile and was very prosperous. His son was very, very ill; no one expected the child to live. Although the nobleman was not a believer, he was so moved by compassion for his son that he found Jesus and asked Him to heal the boy. Jesus didn't respond favorably to his first plea and called the man a sign seeker. But when the nobleman asked Him again, Jesus responded, "*Go your way; your son lives*" (John 4:50).

This child had a serious problem, and his father took his son to Jesus—not physically, but by faith. What do you fathers do when your children have problems? Do you become nervous, start biting your nails, and pull out your hair? No! Do you say, "Oh, I'm letting my wife handle our children"? No!

What happened when that nobleman took his son by faith to Jesus? Jesus spoke the Word, which is God's *transforming power*, and the boy was miraculously healed. And not only was the child healed—the whole family was born again! The *transforming power* of Jesus Christ always does more than we can ask or think. All we need do is to get ahold of God's Word and begin to apply it to our circumstances.

Just hearing Jesus speak the Word increased the nobleman's faith so much that instead of running home to see if his son had been healed, the man went about his business and didn't go home until the next day. He had gotten ahold of God's Word—His *transforming power*—and the man's faith skyrocketed right into the supernatural. He had the faith described in Romans 10:17: *"So then faith comes by hearing, and hearing by the word of God."*

When the nobleman finally went home, his servants rushed out to meet him and said, "Guess what happened? Your son is healed!" The man asked the servants to pinpoint the exact hour when his son had begun to recover. They told him, and he realized that it was the same hour when Jesus had spoken the words of healing. And, you know, just as God's *transforming power* worked in this family, it will work for your family today!

You may think, *Well, my children aren't sick.* But perhaps you suspect your son or daughter is involved in drugs, alcohol, or illicit sex. Or, maybe you have evidence that your children have become involved in the occult. You say, "I've talked to them and done everything I can

think of, but my children won't listen to me." Hang on
and listen to how one man dealt with a similar problem.

A man came to [Jesus], *kneeling down to Him
and saying, "Lord, have mercy on my son, for he
is an epileptic and suffers severely; for he often
falls into the fire and often into the water."*
(Matthew 17:14–15)

Now, this boy had a spiritual need—he needed deliver-
ance. What did Jesus do when He was confronted with
this tormented child, who was under such a tense level
of demon possession that he was falling into fire and water? Did Jesus back off from this boy's problems? No way.

*And Jesus rebuked the demon, and it came out
of him; and the child was cured from that very
hour.* (verse 18)

Jesus spoke the Word and completely turned the
boy's circumstances around, and He'll do the same thing
for your loved ones. You can make the difference in your
loved ones' lives if you will take them by faith to Jesus
and receive His *transforming power* for their situations.

IT'S TIME FOR OUR LOVED ONES TO ARISE

Sometimes, when we read about healings or deliver-
ances, the devil begins to play tricks with our minds.

We find ourselves thinking, *Yeah, Jesus may have been able to handle that situation, but it's not nearly as bad as mine.* Well, let me show you something that will wipe out all your excuses:

> *And behold, one of the rulers of the synagogue came, Jairus by name. And when he saw [Jesus], he fell at His feet and begged Him earnestly, saying, "My little daughter lies at the point of death. Come and lay Your hands on her, that she may be healed, and she will live."* (Mark 5:22–23)

Here we see a father named Jairus coming to Jesus on behalf of his daughter, who was sick almost to the point of death. The name *Jairus* means "he shall enlighten." After his encounter with Jesus, Jairus certainly became enlightened to the *transforming* power of God's Word. He found out that it is never too late for Jesus to turn negative circumstances around.

On His way to heal Jairus's daughter, Jesus stopped to heal a woman who had been hemorrhaging for twelve years. While Jesus was talking to this woman, someone from Jairus's household came and said, *"Your daughter is dead. Why trouble the Teacher any further?"* (Mark 5:35).

Honestly speaking, unless your loved one has died and you are trying to get him resurrected, your problem can't be this bad, can it? I can imagine the utter hopelessness Jairus must have felt when he heard that his precious young daughter had died. He may have thought, *If we hadn't stopped to heal that woman, my daughter might still be alive.*

However, look at Jesus' reaction. Did He break down and start condemning Himself for not being on time to save the girl? No, He began to encourage this distraught father, saying, "Jairus, I know this looks bad, but just keep hanging on to God's *transforming power.*"

When we were in Amarillo, Texas, as assistant pastors, we were involved in prison ministry. Every Sunday afternoon, we would go and preach in the prisons—Wally would minister to the men, and I would minister to the women. One particular Sunday, we had been invited out to dinner by one of the couples in the church. The wife was a new Christian who was just getting ahold of the Word, and her husband was not a Christian. Nevertheless, he had come to church with her that Sunday. We accepted their invitation but told them that we would have to leave right after dinner to fulfill our obligation at the prison. The wife then asked if she and her husband could go with us and watch us minister. We thought that it might be strange to have an unsaved person accompany us to a prison service, but the husband said that he wanted to go, so we told them it was fine with us.

The wife and I finished ministering first, and when we were sitting in the waiting room waiting for Wally and her husband, she said to me, "Marilyn, I know my husband is going to get saved. The Bible says if I believe on the Lord, my house will get saved." She had gotten ahold of God's Word—His transforming power. We had begun to speculate about the different ways through which her husband's salvation might come when the prison chaplain walked in and said, "I've got good news! Pastor Hickey just prayed with your husband, and he received the Lord."

Folks, it doesn't matter when, where, or how God's Word begins to transform our situations, does it? The only thing that matters is that God's Word works! What happened when Jesus arrived at Jairus's house? It was a sad occasion—the house was full of people who were weeping and wailing over his daughter. But *"when [Jesus] came in, He said to them, 'Why make this commotion and weep? The child is not dead, but sleeping'"* (Mark 5:39).

The people began to laugh at Jesus—they thought He was nuts. But it didn't matter to Jesus what they thought. He just made everyone leave the room where the girl was lying, except for His three disciples, Jairus, and his wife. *"Then He took the child by the hand, and said to her, 'Talitha, cumi,' which is translated, 'Little girl, I say to you, arise'"* (verse 41).

Jesus was saying, "Little lamb, it is getting-up time." Doesn't that sound like Jesus? Isn't that just what He would say? Do you remember when your mother used to wake you up when you were little? She'd kiss you and say, "Honey, it's time to get up." Wasn't that just the warmest, sweetest feeling?

What did the young girl do when Jesus spoke the transforming power of God's Word into her spirit? *"Immediately the girl arose and walked, for she was twelve years of age. And they were overcome with great amazement"* (verse 42).

She got up and began to walk around! I can just picture the looks of shock on the faces of all those people who had laughed at Jesus. They were probably stunned to silence!

Parents, put your faith in God's Word—Jesus. Although your children may be dead in trespasses, sins, and all kinds of garbage, you must not let go of God's *transforming power.* Whether your children live at home with

> ***Although your children may be dead in trespasses, sins, and all kinds of garbage, you must not let go of God's transforming power.***

you or on the other side of the world, one day, Jesus is going to say, "Little lamb, little lamb, it's time to rise up out of your sins." And do you know what your little lambs are going to do? That's right—they're going to get up, too. So, be sure to keep on Satan-proofing your family and refuse to let go of God's *transforming power* for their lives.

Just as Jesus told that girl to arise, God is saying to you that it is time for your children to arise out of the defeating lifestyles in which they are operating. It's time for them to be *transformed* into the wonderful vision that God has for them. Did you know that God has made a special promise to you fathers concerning your children? *"He will turn the hearts of the fathers to the children, and the hearts of the children to their fathers, lest I come and strike the earth with a curse"* (Malachi 4:6).

Perhaps your relationships with your children have been strained lately, or, maybe, they're just plain "shot"! Be encouraged because this is a day of enlightenment. Your children aren't going down the drain, no matter what might have transpired in the past. From this day forward, we mothers and fathers are enlightened, and we are going to learn how to deal with our children.

THE MOTHER'S FAITH

We've been looking at the father's faith; now, I want us to look at the mother's faith. There is something unique about a mother's faith that allows her to give her children the benefit of the doubt, no matter how bad the situation may appear. We mothers seem to be equipped with some extra mercy concerning our children, so we can believe that, sooner or later, they are going to come out on top of their circumstances.

The Syrophoenician mother certainly stretched out in supernatural faith on behalf of her hurting daughter:

Then Jesus went out from there and departed to the region of Tyre and Sidon. And behold, a woman of Canaan came from that region and cried out to Him, saying, "Have mercy on me, O Lord, Son of David! My daughter is severely demon-possessed." (Matthew 15:21–22)

This woman's daughter was demon possessed. Your children may not be this troubled, but could they be *influenced* by what they watch on television? Have you ever monitored the programs that your children like to watch? Do you know what kinds of values they are developing based upon the immoral lifestyles of certain characters portrayed on television? Folks, become more involved with your children so that Satan won't be able to pick them off like ducks at a shooting gallery. Your children are your fruit, so make sure that they learn how to be valuable to themselves, as well as to others.

> *Your children are your fruit, so make sure that they learn how to be valuable to themselves, as well as to others.*

This desperate mother who sought Jesus' help said that her daughter was *"severely demon-possessed."* The spirits possessing this girl were hurting her, and she needed to be set free. The devil was hurting that poor girl then, and he is still hurting people today. Living a lifestyle beneath that which God has destined for us *hurts!*

So, the woman came to Jesus, but *"He answered her not a word. And His disciples came and urged Him, saying, 'Send her away, for she cries out after us.' But He answered and said, 'I was not sent except to the lost sheep of the house of Israel'"* (Matthew 15:23–24).

I love this woman's tenacity. She easily could have been offended by Jesus and the disciples and walked away. But, instead, she came closer and began to worship Jesus. She said, *"Lord, help me!"* (verse 25). *"But He answered and said, 'It is not good to take the children's bread and throw it to the little dogs.' And she said, 'Yes, Lord, yet even the little dogs eat the crumbs which fall from their masters' table'"* (verses 26–27).

Jesus actually called her a dog! But did she turn away and run home crying? No! She was determined to get ahold of Jesus Christ, the living Word—God's *transforming power*—for her daughter! She was not about to let anything stop her, and she got the victory for her daughter. *"Then Jesus answered and said to her, 'O woman, great is your faith! Let it be to you as you desire.' And her daughter was healed from that very hour"* (verse 28).

Offenses are deliberate traps that have been laid by the devil, and if you're not very careful, you'll fall into one of these traps and miss your miracle. Perhaps indignation would be the natural response to some situation, but it's your choice as to whether you are going to operate in the natural (your old nature) or the supernatural (your new nature). The woman Jesus was talking with *chose* not to become offended by the way Jesus treated her and by the rudeness of His disciples. She *chose* not to be offended, even when Jesus called her a dog. Rather, she humbled herself and said, "Lord, if I am a dog, I am Your dog, and I want the crumbs that fall from Your table."

Years ago, a man with a marvelous miracle ministry came to our church. He really led a consecrated life and fasted and prayed so much that he looked like a pile of bones. There were always many miracles when he came, but there also were many people who were offended by him. Our telephone at the church would ring off the hook with people calling to say, "He is so crude." And he was. I remember one night, he said to a woman, "What are you doing up here tonight? I prayed for you last night. Sit down!" She kind of crept off the stage and sat down, and she missed her miracle. But do you know that the people who hung in there and refused to become offended experienced many miracles in their lives?

Now, don't get me wrong; I am not saying that this man was right to be so offensive. I don't really know what his problem was, but I do know that the people who allowed themselves to be offended by his crude personality really missed out on their miracles.

Power to Transform the Past

God's transforming power can correct situations that may result from improper parenting.

The fourth thing I want you to understand is that God's transforming power can correct situations that may result from improper parenting. Let's face it: no matter how good our intentions are, we parents sometimes promote failure rather than faith in our children.

One day, my son Mike said to me, "Mother, if you and Dad had put half as much into me as you put into Sarah, I would be much further down the road." I almost responded defensively, "Well, Michael, we tried, but you really botched it up sometimes, and we had a very hard time dealing with you.

But the Lord said, "Don't do that; don't be defensive at all. Just admit where you blew it." So, instead of reading my son the riot act, I said, "Michael, you're right; there were things that we did wrong. Can you find it in your heart to forgive us?" He said, "Of course, I do."

Perhaps you have made some mistakes in raising your children. But is God going back on His word just because you may have blown it? No, because God's *transforming power* can undo any mistakes we may have made in raising our children. Although it was certainly unintentional, I failed my son in some areas, but I never failed to love him. And I know that God is going to bring Michael through, despite my mistakes.

There was a little boy born in Egypt who, if not for his mother's faith, never would have achieved God's goal for his life: "*So the woman conceived and bore a son. And when she saw that he was a beautiful child, she hid him three months*" (Exodus 2:2). The Hebrew word for "*beautiful*" can also mean "prosperous, and excellent"—that's what this baby's mother saw when she looked into his tiny face. All babies are beautiful to their own mothers, right? I've never heard a mother say, "I've got the ugliest baby in the world." Have you? The baby may have big ears or a big nose, and most newborns look kind of beat up. But, to his mother, every baby is absolutely beautiful.

I don't blame Jochebed one bit for refusing using to allow her son to be killed because of some stupid Egyptian law: "*So Pharaoh commanded all his people, saying, 'Every son who is born you shall cast into the river, and every daughter you shall save alive'*" (Exodus 1:22).

Jochebed really had a mother's faith for her baby. She hid him for three months; then, she put him in an ark and placed him in the bullrushes near the place that

Pharaoh's daughter bathed. When Pharaoh's daughter found the baby, she had compassion on him. She named the baby Moses—which means "drawing out"—took him home, and raised him as her own son.

Because of his mother's faith, Moses' life was spared, and he was highly educated and had the best of everything. After some really serious learning experiences, Moses, at eighty years of age, answered God's call upon his life to deliver the Israelites out of Egypt.

Looking back on the circumstances surrounding Moses' birth, would you have foreseen all of this in his future? I doubt it. But God's transforming power turned Moses' life around. So, instead of being killed instantly at birth or becoming dinner for a bunch of hungry crocodiles, Moses became the deliverer of Israel.

When we compare Moses' situation to what we may be experiencing, we can say that not all Christian parents were born again at early age. Some of us spent a lot of years living in sinful lifestyles; therefore, our children were raised in ungodly homes and may have had difficult lives. Regardless of their beginnings, though, God has plans for your children—they may even be future deliverers in the body of Christ. So, stop feeling guilty about any mistakes you may have made in parenting your children. Seek God and repent. Then, ask your children to forgive you, and stand on God's Word—His transforming power for their lives.

CATCH THE FAITH VISION

The last thing I want you to consider is catching God's faith vision for your children. Often, we see reflections of ourselves and our spouses when we look at our children. And that's okay—as long as the traits we see are in accord with God's will. However, what happens when we or our spouses have been involved in alcohol abuse, drug addiction, or other destructive habits? How about your children? Have you caught a glimpse of God's faith vision? Don't look at what is occurring in the natural; see your loved ones by faith!

> **Don't look at what is occurring in the natural; see your loved ones by faith!**

I can remember when Mike used to come by the church while he was high on drugs. He was so pitiful. But, one day, God showed me how to catch His faith vision for my son. I would envision Mike with a Bible in his hands, praising the Lord—that's how God saw him when he looked at my son. Then, one summer night, I saw Mike standing in the back of the church with his hands lifted high in the air; and he was singing in tongues. Praise God! His faith vision had been manifested from the spiritual realm into the natural realm.

Folks, hold on to God's *transforming power* and begin to see what God sees when He looks at your loved ones. God never called believers to be conformers, right? We are here to be *transformers* so that we can subdue the earth, which is what He put us here to do in the first place.

I want you to know that I am praying for every one of you to begin to take authority over your circumstances. That's what God has destined for all people: "*So God created man in His own image,...and God said to them, 'Be fruitful and multiply; fill the earth and subdue it'*" (Genesis 1:27, 28).

God does not want your family to become another statistic in the "failure of the family" epidemic. If you will take the precautions I have been talking about for guarding yourself and your home against Satan's divisive elements, then your family will not give way to the force of his storms. By faith, I am standing with you in prayer. God has commissioned *you* to be a Satan-proofer, and, from this day forward, the devil doesn't have a chance in your home!

Receive Jesus Christ
as Lord and Savior of Your Life

The Bible says,

That if you confess with your mouth the Lord Jesus and believe in your heart that God has raised Him from the dead, you will be saved. For with the heart one believes unto righteousness, and with the mouth confession is made unto salvation. (Romans 10:9–10)

To receive Jesus Christ as Lord and Savior of your life, sincerely pray this prayer from your heart:

Dear Jesus,

I believe that You died for me and that You rose again on the third day. I confess to You that I am a sinner and that I need Your love and forgiveness. Come into my life, forgive my sins, and give me eternal life. I confess You now as my Lord. Thank You for my salvation!

Signed,

_____

Date

_____

About the Author

As founder and president of Marilyn Hickey Ministries, Marilyn is being used by God to help cover the earth with the Word. Her Bible teaching ministry is an international outreach via television, satellite, books, CDs, DVDs, and healing meetings. Marilyn has established an international program of Bible and food distribution, and she is committed to overseas ministry, often bringing the gospel to people who have never heard it before.

Marilyn's message of encouragement to all believers emphasizes the fact that today can be the best day of your life if Jesus Christ is living in you. In addition to ministering, Marilyn is a busy wife, the mother of two grown children, five grandchildren, and four great-grandchildren. She and her husband, Wallace Hickey, are the founding pastors of Orchard Road Christian Center in Greenwood Village, Colorado.